My Life Is a Situation Comedy

by

Bill Persky

To Patricia

my spirit freind

Bill

Printed in the United States of America

Mandevilla Press.,7 Indian Valley Rd. Weston, CT 06883

MANDEVILLA
PRESS

First Edition: April 2012

ISBN: 978-1-62704-000-6

Library of Congress Cataloging-in-Publication Data pending

Starring

Marlo Thomas Carl Reiner Orson Welles My Mother
Dick Van Dyke My First Wife Mary Tyler Moore Bill Cosby
Steve Allen Goldie Hawn Peter Sellers My Second Wife
Susan St. James & Jane Curtin My Father
Fred Astaire & Gene Kelly My Southern Belle Tim Conway
The Smothers Brothers My Three Daughters My Sister Bunny
Andy Williams Cary Grant
Joanna

AND MANY MORE!!!

Dedication

To my wife Joanna

For always being……Joanna.

A GOOD WORD
ABOUT THE AUTHOR

I daresay that had Bill Persky not come into my life in 1963, I would most certainly not be here today writing a heartfelt and glowing foreword to this highly entertaining memoir. Back then, I was beside myself with worry about being capable of continuing on, all alone, as the producer/writer of The Dick Van Dyke Show. Now that I think about it, had I not rejected a premise for a Dick Van Dyke Show episode that Billy and his partner Sam Denoff offered me...and had Billy not doggedly applied himself to turning it into a speculative script ... and had I not succumbed to Billy's plaintive begging ... and had I not reluctantly agreed to read their second attempt at writing a script ... and had that second attempt not turned out to be one of the best episodes we ever filmed ... Well, Billy, coming along when he did, saved my life.

In the following pages, Billy Persky writes about his life and career and gives me far too much credit for his success. I am proud of the fact that I have had a hand in his career, and for the past 50 years, his situation comedy life. I once described Billy as always looking for the world's greatest burger – and constantly finding it. His great weakness is his boundless enthusiasm, and I hope he never loses it. I hope you have as much fun reading what follows as I did.

-- **Carl Reiner**

AND JUST A FEW MORE …..

Bill Persky's writing is exactly what you would expect from one of the most accomplished comedy writers in show business... brilliant!

From his auspicious start producing infomercials to the sitcoms we all love which earned him five Emmys, Billy takes a hilarious look at success, failure, triumph, divorce, children, marriage, and even death with heart, soul and humor. Billy is such a descriptive storyteller, I feel like I was there! You will too! Instructions for a good time: Read Bill Persky's book. Laugh and repeat.

-- Kelly Ripa

Billy Persky's life has been one long and beautiful love-fest -- he loves writing, he loves women, and he loves laughter -- and this marvelous memoir captures every touching and funny step along that journey. I read it with tears in my eyes and a warm feeling in my heart. You will, too.

-- Marlo Thomas

Bill Persky guided me through the wonderful world of half hour comedy, keeping me laughing and well fed along the way. He'll make you feel happy and well fed too. He's a wonderful story teller. Taste!

-- Jane Curtin

MY LIFE IS A SITUATION COMEDY is a funny, wonderful primer on a life lived well, equal parts love and humor. I am just thrilled that as Kate in KATE & ALLIE that I got to be a "situation" in Billy's comedy.

-- Susan Saint James

For more than thirty years I have lived with a woman who loves another man: Bill Persky (she calls him *Billy*). Having read his book, I finally see why.

 -- **Phil Donahue**

Bill Persky is the man behind some of my all-time favorite TV shows. He's also hilarious, and appreciates women. That's my kind of guy - and his book is full of my kind of stories, hilarious!

-- **Andy Cohen**

FOREWORD

By the Author

Don't get the wrong idea. I have had my fair share of *situations* involving loss, pain, failure, disappointment, illness, and disaster. The *comedy* comes from watching myself, in disbelief, as I attempt to make things right and maintain a semblance of dignity while constantly slipping on the banana peels of life.

Many of my slips ended up as episodes of *The Dick Van Dyke Show, That Girl, Kate & Allie,* and over 300 other TV shows and films. What follows is my personal Situation Comedy, which played out while you were watching them.

The stories that follow are all true, but some of the names have been changed to protect the privacy of those who might not wish to be identified. Others are too close, important or famous to be called anything but who they are.

BACKSTORY

The *backstory* is an important step in the creation of any sitcom; it is how the characters got to be the lovable, flawed, and predictable people we watch and love—or hate—while usually finding something of ourselves in them, something we are, or we want to be.

My backstory, in brief, was of a kid brought up during The Depression, which my parents considered an emotional as well as financial condition.

The Emotional Depression never came to an end. My father was "on the road" a lot, doing anything to earn a buck, from being a circus barker to a vegetable peeler pitchman—a real life Willie Loman who finally achieved success, if not fulfillment, as the owner of an auction gallery in Atlantic City.

His backstory—that of a poor, Orthodox Jewish family in Holyoke, Massachusetts —never gave him a chance to realize his true potential or his dreams. He was humorless, judgmental, hypocritical, and, frankly, not missed a lot since I had the full attention of my mother: a warm, funny, but anxiety-ridden woman who kept things together through bad times and worse as we moved from relative to relative and town to town. One moment of Christmas, 1934, when I was three, stays with me and sets the tone for a lifelong questioning of my sense of reality, and would ever after play an important part in my complex relationships with women.

A Santa Claus came to our apartment, a cold-water flat in East Orange, New Jersey, and let me choose a toy from his bag. I picked a wooden milk wagon with yellow sides and a red roof pulled by a black-and-white spotted horse. I couldn't have been happier until I went to show it to my mother who was crying. How could something that made me so happy make her so sad? What was wrong with my perception? I started to cry along with her, trusting she knew something I didn't. Although she never told me, I came to realize that the gift was from the welfare people, and my sense of joy was hers of shame. There are countless examples of this dynamic that set up my constant uncertainty in trusting my own sense of reality, especially where women were concerned.

My father's constant absence made me the man of the house, certainly before I was ready. I clearly remember when I was 6, the landlord came to collect the overdue rent, and my mother's embarrassment standing there taking his insulting harangue until she was brought to tears. Without hesitation I hurled all 3 feet 32 pounds of me at him, punching and kicking as we fell down the stairs, where I was finally pulled off by his wife and son. "Save the woman" was part of my DNA.

During the famed 1938 Orson Welles *War of the Worlds* radio hoax that panicked the entire nation, my sister and I were home alone listening: I was 7 and she was 14, yet I felt it was up to me to protect her as we ran into the street, expecting to face the Martian invaders. "Save the women" and "trust the woman before yourself" was a combination that led to a life-long search for how to deal with them, and to countless outlandish situations and a lot of the comedy.

I am kind of a Peter Sellers character around women, someone who is always seemingly in charge, yet who has no idea what he is doing. Which—even though this is out of sequence—I had a chance to observe in Mr. Sellers firsthand.

REHAB, HERE I COME

Very aware that I had an addictive personality when it came to everything from ice cream to M&Ms, I always knew to approach drugs and alcohol with extreme caution.

The alcohol was not a great threat because I had such a low tolerance that, after two drinks, I was looking for a lampshade. Drugs were another issue, and I decided to avoid them all together, managing to do so until October 10, 1969, a day I can't really remember but will never forget.

My partner, Sam Denoff, and I (henceforth to be known as "us" or "we") arrived in London that morning after an overnight flight from Los Angeles to present our ideas for Goldie Hawn's first television special, *Pure Goldie*, which we were writing and producing. *Laugh-In* had made her a superstar, and she was in London filming the screen version of *There's a Girl in My Soup* with Peter Sellers. Like everyone else, Sellers had fallen in love with Goldie and had tentatively agreed to be her guest on the special. It was a great coup, and we had come to London to dazzle him and clinch the deal.

We arrived exhausted after a 14-hour flight, having left Los Angeles at noon and landing at Heathrow at ten the next morning. The over-the-pole flight was an ordeal eased only by the free-flowing champagne, vodka, and caviar, which resulted in our sorry condition upon arrival. We were met by Edmond, a very British agent from William Morris, who informed us that we had a meeting with Goldie and Sellers at 1 p.m. to run through the show. Although the material was in great shape, we obviously weren't, and we debated whether to take a two-hour nap or just push through and hope for the best. Jolly old Edmond had a better solution and produced a little blue pill.

It was a Dexamyl, which you can think of as being the Ecstasy of the 60s—combining an upper with a downer: taking you there and back in one easy swallow.

Neither of us were pill takers, but Edmond assured us there was no risk and it would help us carry the day. We refused, but he insisted we keep it—"Just in case"—as he dropped us at the Connaught, one of the truly great London hotels, meaning old and very proper. (Marlo Thomas had wanted us to stay there when we visited her for a meeting on the pilot of *That Girl*, but we couldn't get in.) This time we were more fortunate (or, arguably, less, as we entered the lobby, which reminded me of my grandmother's house). We were about to turn around and leave for the Hilton until the elevator door opened revealing two of England's greatest movie stars: David Niven and Rex Harrison.

We decided to stay.

After a lot of coffee and cold showers, we sat in our room staring into space and dropping off into fitful moments of sleep, one of which was interrupted when the door slowly opened and a tiny man dressed in tails and older than the hotel silently walked across the room to the mantle where there was a clock even older than him. He took a key from a chain around his neck, wound the clock, and silently exited. If we both hadn't seen it, I would have thought I was hallucinating, but somehow it helped us realize that if we were to make it through the meeting, one of us should use the pill. Because Sam had a slight heart condition, I took half and we went to meet Goldie and Sellers.

In the cab Sam looked at me apprehensively, waiting for some sign of change. I felt nothing and considered the possibility that Edmond had given me a dud. But in the elevator that dud kicked in, and by the time we got to Goldie's suite, I was way beyond awake with my heart rate at about 300, my eyes open so wide I feared they might fall out, and my foot tapping uncontrollably. I said a quick hello—probably *too* quick—and went into the bathroom to calm down while Sam, in a more relaxed mood, set the stage for our presentation. I don't remember what happened next, but, according to Sam, it was spectacular.

Apparently, I went into a non-stop performance of the show: dancing, singing, doing all the sketches and even orchestral interludes. I went on like this for about 40 minutes, and when I was finished singing the final number, both Goldie and Sellers applauded. He agreed to do the show, and Sam ushered me out, not knowing what I might do next.

When we got into the elevator, Sam gave me a hug and said I had been fantastic. At that point, I started to cry, which I did uncontrollably through the very staid lobby of the Berkeley, in the cab to our hotel, through the even more staid lobby of The Connaught, and for the next three hours.

Goldie called full of compliments, saying Peter loved us and wanted to celebrate our deal at dinner. I was physically exhausted and mentally on the edge, but who could give up dinner with Peter Sellers? I wondered if I should take the other half of the pill so that he wouldn't be disappointed with the real me.

We showered again, changed our clothes again, and, still without sleep, went off to an elegant Japanese restaurant where Sellers had reserved a private room. As a sign of how special he thought we were, he was going to bring along his latest girlfriend. Again I considered taking the other half of the pill, sure I had become an addict, and was already anticipating rehab.

We arrived first and were shown to a screened tatami room. A beautiful Japanese woman removed our shoes while another brought us warm towels and sake, and we reclined on the floor, comforted by cushions. It was all I could do to keep from curling up and going to sleep, so when Sam went to the men's room, I took a nibble out of the other half of the blue pill—just enough to keep me awake.

And then Sellers arrived with...*her.*

I knew he had a reputation for dating beautiful women, but nothing could prepare you for *her*. Beauty was the least of it: she was elegant, haughty, imperious and delightful. And that was just as she walked toward us from the entrance. She was also Lady Somebody, the madcap daughter of some extension of the royal family. She was dressed in whatever the 60s London fashion world had agreed was the perfect look for the day: a miniskirt and a pair of thigh-high leopard lace-up boots, which took her about ten minutes to unlace.

Fortunately, Goldie arrived shortly after because my latest reaction to the pill was a heightened sense of awareness, and I found myself aware that Lady Evelyn wasn't thrilled at being there—or anywhere—with Sellers. As it turned out, this was the last night of their relationship, and, from what I saw, there never should have been a first.

They seemed to have nothing in common but their commitment to the fact that she was wonderful. And she was! That she managed to treat him and us with complete disdain and still come off as charming and delightful is something the English can pull off and we Americans can't. The charm and delight lasted through two rounds of sake, the tempura and soup, but by the main course it was over.

By then, I was in a kind of agitated stupor so I don't recall exactly what provoked it, but the restaurant came to a standstill as she suddenly erupted and declared that she was leaving. Sellers went into a medley of every inept lover he had played on screen with "My darling, my darling" preceding everything he tried to say.

The high—and the low—point was her exit. In a performance worthy of Chaplin, Keaton, Laurel & Hardy, and, of course, Inspector Clouseau, as she was trying to run her boot laces around the dozens of little hooks on her leopard boots, he was on his knees pleading, managing to somehow get his hands and necktie caught up in her laces. It would have been a lot simpler for her to just pick the boots up and walk out barefoot, but I guess a Lady doesn't do that, so she kept lacing and swearing as he kept pleading. Finally, with the boots partially laced and Sellers completely bound up in them, she made a most un-Ladylike trudge to the exit, dragging him behind her, an action that I found hilarious and, so, I broke into gales of laughter, followed by a repeat of my crying.

For some reason, Peter Sellers was not Goldie's guest on the special, and I never took another pill given to me by an agent. *Note: Though I have lived my life sequentially, it's not remembered that way. One thing reminds me of another and that leads to yet another, so I will follow where the memories take me, but since this is about my life in the entertainment business, I'll start with what led me there, and in the end, the punch line, as usual, involved a woman.*

BUSBY BERKLEY PRESENTS

If one day of my life should have been a Hollywood musical, it was Sunday, September 23, 1953. It would star Donald O'Connor. I'd prefer Gene Kelly, but he was too graceful, strong, and heroic to play the jerk I was that day. Actually, "jerk" doesn't really capture it, but I'm trying to avoid Jewish words to make this whole story more universal. Were that not the case, the word of choice would be "schmuck."

There is some disagreement as to what makes one a "schmuck," leading to an ongoing dialogue occupying linguistic scholars for centuries as to whether it is interchangeable with "putz." The prevailing opinion is as follows:

A "schmuck" is one who climbs a ladder with too many things in his hands, wearing leather-soled shoes, during a snowstorm, with a high fever, and reaches one rung too high, bringing the ladder and himself crashing to earth.

The person holding the ladder—the one he lands on—is a "putz."

That point thus clarified, I think a more proper description of me that day is "asshole," which includes all of the above and, I would think, requires little further clarification.

I was fresh out of Syracuse University where I had majored in fun, and my sole ambition for the future was to not be in my father's business. He owned an auction gallery on the boardwalk in pre-gambling Atlantic City and there was nothing about the business or Atlantic City that appealed to me, and because I had majored in advertising, I was off to New York where my cousin, Lester, owned a small agency. Nepotism was pushed to the limit as I was taken on at a salary of $25 a week for a menial job for which I still managed to be highly under-qualified.

I bought the summer uniform of the day: snap-brimmed straw hat with madras band, seersucker suit, and an attaché case, this last being essential to carry the Danish and sandwiches that were part of my job description. I was euphemistically titled a "trainee," and as for my assignments, tasks, responsibilities, functions, duties -- actually, the crap I handled included running errands, running the switchboard, running the ditto machine (remember those? I *still* have purple stains on my hands), running the supply room, running the. . . Well, if running was involved, I did it. Although coveralls would have been more realistic apparel, I wore that seersucker and hat every day to be dressed for my Big Break into the world of non-janitorial activity—should it ever arrive.

When that break came three weeks later, it literally *was* a break, particularly that of the left ankle of the production assistant in the TV department. As the "trainee" – and since there were only four people in the company, two of them being partners – I was not only next in line for his job, I was the *only* one in that line.

Our biggest account was the Roto Broil 400, a countertop cooking unit that could roast, toast, broil, boil, bake, fry and rotisserie all at the same time (whether you wanted it to or not). Ron Popeil is still selling them. They were big in the early 50s, and all the major companies made them—G.E., Philco, KitchenAid— but Roto Broil, a small independent manufacturer, was leading the pack mainly due to the marketing genius of Cousin Lester.

Although he isn't given credit (maybe that should

be blame), Lester invented the infomercial. He came up with a 15-minute cooking show using the Roto Broil, called "The Roto Magician," gave it to stations around the country, and took a free one-minute "call-in" pitch in return. It was brilliant. Since all the food was roasted, toasted, broiled, boiled, baked, fried and rotisseried on the Roto Broil, the whole show was, in effect, a commercial.

Our "chef" was an ex-carnival pitchman whose previous culinary expertise was limited to eating out. Still, he looked like a pro since he'd been pitching peelers, slicers, dicers, juicers, shredders, graters, and other kitchen gadgets on the boardwalk in Atlantic City. He was a brilliant salesman and as good at slicing, dicing, and shredding as the Roto Broil was at roasting, toasting, and broiling, et cetera. The show was magical, and the food looked great, largely due to the coating of shellac we applied so everything glistened under the lights.

My entry into TV production was as auspicious as it was unexpected. It happened so suddenly that when I got to the studio I still had Cousin Lester's bologna sandwich in my attaché case. That evening was to be Roto Broil's first night sponsoring *The Ernie Kovacs Show*, the biggest thing on New York late night TV. It was also the *only* show on New York late night TV since most stations signed off at midnight with the "The Star-Spangled Banner." For Cousin Lester's little agency, this was a step into the big time, and my cousin understandably wanted a major production. This was live TV with no rehearsal, and I was yanked right from the ditto machine, purple hands and all, to produce the whole thing.

The plan was for The Roto Magician to arrive at the studio entrance in the Roto Broil 18-wheeler. Ernie Kovacs would climb some steps, open the rear truck doors to welcome him to the show, and the two would walk, with great fanfare, along a plush red carpet into the studio. I was to be in the truck holding the Roto Magician in place with one arm, a Roto Broil under the other, which I had to hand out to him without being seen on camera as the door opened. Because the interior of the trailer was in total darkness, I also had to hold a flashlight on the door. With both hands and arms taken, in a decision worthy of the logistical genius of Steven Spielberg, I put the flashlight in my mouth.

When the countdown started, I was nervous but confident as I waited with Roto Magician's hand in my right hand, Roto Broil in my left, and flashlight in my mouth. This was it! My first step into the world of show business! They gave me a headset and I was so excited I made an acceptance speech, thanking all the people who had helped me get there.

"Three, two, one…"

This was *IT!*

The door handle turned and I was on, steadying the Magician into place as the door swung open. In one fluid move I led him to the steps, handed him the broiler and dived out of sight while switching off the flashlight with my tongue.

On landing, a perfect tuck and roll brought me to my feet. Everything had gone off flawlessly. Waiting in the darkness, I ran scenarios of how to play the whole thing when the doors opened and Cousin Lester was waiting to congratulate me on a job well done. Deciding on an attitude of absolute cool with loosened tie and hat tipped rakishly back, I struck a Sinatra-like pose at the truck door.

Suddenly, I was catapulted into the air and flying backward as the truck lurched forward. In total darkness, with nothing to hold onto, I crashed hard into the rear door. I struggled to my feet only to be hurtled forward through the darkness as the truck came to an abrupt stop. I couldn't for the life of me figure out what was happening, but after a few more crashing starts and stops, I realized the "life of me" definitely was at stake! On the next flight forward, I managed to grab some webbing as I crashed into the front wall. Screaming and pounding seemed like a good idea and I was doing both as we took off again, this time for a long, uninterrupted run. Obviously the driver was headed somewhere, and if it was more than a few stops and starts, I'd be dead by the time he got there.

After about ten minutes I had given up hope of survival when we stopped yet again, and, as I crashed into the forward wall, it appeared the motor had been turned off. I say *appeared*, because I could have just been dead and beyond hearing. Then, the sound of the driver's door slamming was a sign not only that I was still alive, but also that we *had* actually stopped.

Great!

Well, not so great.

I was still only semiconscious and locked in the back of a truck only God knew where. After weighing my options, I went back to pounding and screaming, augmented by crying and praying. The combination eventually worked as the door opened and the driver—accompanied by two cops, guns drawn—peered in. They discovered a lump of cuts and bruises wrapped in what had once been a seersucker suit (I never did find the hat). The driver had had no idea anyone had been back there, and, fortunately for me – and whoever would have cleaned the truck – this stop for coffee was the last until he got to Baltimore.

From that point, my rise in the company was meteoric. Not only had I shown courage and ingenuity, but also Cousin Lester was really impressed I hadn't filed for Workmen's Comp. I did consider asking for a new hat, but why be petty?

The promotion to junior executive entitled me to do all my previous jobs plus countless new ones. Overnight, I went from "trainee" at $25 for a five-day week to assistant producer at $25 for seven.

Working weekends during the summer was not a glorious prospect, but I ended up loving it. The Roto Magician was on WPIX Sunday afternoon at 3 o'clock, and by the end of the summer I was doing it all: writing, menu planning, shopping, shellacking the food. I even had a credit as producer. By September 23rd, I was still earning $25 a week, but filled with self-importance and only one step from referring to myself in the third person.

That particular Sunday was one of those days in New York (there's one each season) when all the elements combine to create a perfect version of that time of year. This was the one perfect fall day: 70 degrees with just a whisper of a breeze, radiant sun parked in a flawless version of the color blue, air so clean the edges of the buildings were razor sharp. People were using the day to its full potential: picnics in the park, ballgames of every description, strolling and drinking in the day.

On my way to the studio, I envied their freedom. But when you're in show business, there are no hours, no seasons— just the show. The world needed the Roto Magician and only *I* could bring it to them. Maybe it was the long hours and no time off, and to the rest of the world, it was only a 15-minute cooking show, but to me it was The Greatest Story Ever Told. Obviously, I was losing touch with reality.

I got to the studio and loved the camaraderie, even everyone bitching about working on such a beautiful day. But I knew they'd be proud to be part of the show I had planned: on the rotisserie spit was chicken roasting (with glitter blended into the shellac for extra highlights), French bread toasting, baby onions broiling, Brussels sprouts boiling, new potatoes baking, and apple fritters frying. When the show ended, the answering service phones lit up with orders, and Cousin Lester called to tell me he was hiring a new trainee.

I left the studio walking on air. From never giving much thought to what life after college would be and not really prepared to do much, I was on my way to an incredibly joyous and successful career. But all I could know that day was that this job was something I loved doing, in a place where I loved living, on a day I loved being a part of.

Dressed in khakis, a white shirt, loafers, and a sweater tied casually over my shoulders, I started walking, almost dancing, home. The world was a stage and I was on it. If it had been raining, I would have been singing in it. Everyone passing by had a smile for me, which I returned. Along the way was an old lady needing help across the street, lost tourists needing directions, a blind man looking for an address, and countless guys looking for a handout. I was there for all of them, and, with each, I managed to get in some version of what a day it had been for me.

The blind man was easy. "Yeah, beautiful day—you can't see it of course—hey, neither could I, locked away in the studio, doing the show, all that pressure. But, look, I'm not complaining. It's the life I chose."

With the old lady shuffling on her canes (or crutches): "Take your time, ma'am, I have all day. Hey, it's a pleasure just to be outside after that drab studio all day, doing the show, all that pressure. But look, I'm not complaining. It's the life I chose." Her pace seemed to quicken as I spoke.

I found the lost tourists difficult given that they didn't speak English, but pantomime helped.

I assured the panhandlers their lives would turn around, and yet, in a way, I envied their freedom: "No cares, no responsibilities, not being stuck in a studio all day. But, look, I'm not complaining. It's the life I chose."

A stop at a grocery store for a quart of milk gave me a chance to explain to the young Puerto Rican clerk that we were brothers under the skin through our shared, working-Sunday experience. He shook his head knowingly in agreement—or self-defense, figuring I was some kind of lunatic. And I was! I know it now, and I'm sure I did then. But I was caught up in the moment, so I just enjoyed it.

It only got out of hand after I left the grocery. I sensed people taking notice of me as we passed and assumed my inner glow was creating some kind of aura. On a less ethereal level, what they were taking notice of was the leaking milk carton creating a suspicious wet spot on the fly of my pants. Of course I was oblivious as I continued on in the zone of grandiosity I had created. The world was mine, and I wished I could just let Ellen Kresky know how wrong she had been about me.

We had been pinned in college (do they still do that?). The relationship was very 50s with a lot of window-steamed petting in the front seat of my Pontiac Catalina. It was a given we would marry after graduation and for Ellen's family there was no doubt what the future held. Her father owned a very successful garment business and he loved me. . . I think more than she did. I was the son he never had and, thusly, the one to take over the business.

A father-in-law's business was no more appealing to me than a father's, and I think my lack of enthusiasm for the arrangement was as much a part of the "un-pinning" as anything else. I took a stand, making a speech that my future was an open book and I would fill the pages with wonders and adventures the garment industry could never afford. Because I was on academic probation at the time, nobody gave much credence to my predictions.

But now here I was, just a few short months later an *Assistant Producer* of the Roto Magician, earning $25 a week, parading down Sixth Avenue with a growing wet spot on my fly. "Oh, if they could see me now!"

Then, as I crossed 57th and Sixth, in a moment worthy of *On the Town*, I spotted Ellen's cousin, Sheila. Actually, if it had happened in a movie, you wouldn't believe it! It was *too* perfect, but I didn't hesitate to make the most of it.

When Sheila saw me, I sensed what I took to be amazement, but was, in fact, terror. I don't know how much the milk spot – which now appeared as if I had completely lost all bladder control – affected her, but she was transfixed. We embraced—or at least *I* did. After dealing with the coincidence— "What a surprise!"—and how good we both looked, I waited for an opportunity to tell her (knowing she'd tell Ellen) how great I was doing.

There was an awkward pause, and then she said, "Sooooo," which was just the opening I needed.

"Sooooo, I'm on my way home from work. I know it's Sunday, but that's how it is in this business. It's a pleasure to just be outside after being stuck in that studio all day, doing the show, all that pressure. But, look, I'm not complaining. It's the life I chose."

Her response of "Uh-huh" indicated she wanted more detail.

"Oh, yeah, it's a grind, but they don't pay this kind of money for nothing—you have to deliver. But, hey, I'm not complaining. It's the life I chose. So how's Ellen?"

She managed a stunned, "Fine."

I returned a condescending, "Hey, that's great. I always knew she would be fine. Great girl, and I'm sorry things didn't work out for us, but, hey, you have to follow your star." Not wanting to overplay the moment, I gave her a peck on the cheek and, I'm appalled to admit, a *"Ciao!"* as I left. I never looked back as I affected a walk combining confidence, success, potential, self-esteem and humility. That's a lot to put into a walk, but I'd been working on it all summer and pretty much had it down. Turning the corner on 59th Street I started to giggle. What a break! Ellen would be impressed, heartbroken, and would tell everyone from school I had already made it big.

By now, I realized the milk had saturated my left pant leg, and, at the same moment I also noticed a large crowd in front of the Hampshire House staring horror-struck in my direction. I turned to see what was behind me, and, finding nothing unusual, turned back to realize they were staring at *me!*

I'm sure the wet pants looked silly and might provoke laughter, but why *horror?* Who were these people?

Wait a minute…

I *knew* these people: Jim and Jodi Riess, Donnie and Ellen Rosen, Lou and Cindy, Kyle and Lila, Tony, Eric…There must have been 50 people, and I knew all of them from school!

What a break! A new audience for what, by now, I had honed into a masterpiece of self-aggrandizement. If Cousin Rita didn't tell Ellen, this group surely would!

In a bizarre turn of events, I got the opportunity to tell her myself as she, the joyous bride led by her adoring groom, emerged from the hotel, prepared for a shower of rice on their way to the limo waiting at the curb.

For a moment everything was slow motion because the situation was too much to deal with in real time. It was beyond impossible, and yet there I was, in my milk-sodden pants, face to face with my ex-girlfriend and her new husband, surrounded by all of our friends who broke the tension by starting to throw rice. I probably left a few things out, but that should be enough to set the scene.

Since dying or falling through a hole in the ground wasn't an option, I did the next best thing: my impression of Cary Grant saying, "Ellen, Ellen, Ellen." Having heard she was getting married to a guy named Ted, I assumed the guy in tails was him and followed with, "Ted, Ted, Ted." By now, the rice, clinging to the milk on my pants, was starting to expand along with everyone's embarrassment.

Stupidity loves a vacuum, so I defused the awkwardness by getting between the newlyweds, arm over both their shoulders, and escorting them to their limo. Nobody wanted to upset me given that the leaking bag I carried could well have been a bomb. Reaching the car, I opened the door, wished them well, and asked where they were going on their honeymoon. They probably thought I was planning to join them. Of course it was Bermuda, which, in the 50s was almost a requirement for your marriage to be official. I could have let it go at that, but didn't.

"Wow! Bermuda! Great! Of course, I'd be happy to go anywhere just to get away from the grind. In the studio, even on Sunday, but, hey, I'm not complaining. It's the life I chose—" and, in one final attempt to come off as a hero "—and a life I love and am doing well at."

I showed real class by leaving out, "Good luck in the garment business, Ted."

They drove off and I stood for a moment not wanting to turn and face the crowd that had been watching. When I did, I saved the moment with a Porky Pig, "Tha-tha-tha-tha-tha-that's all, folks!" followed by my best version of Charlie Chaplin walking off into his next adventure.

IS ROCCO THERE?

The early 50s was a great time to get started as a comedy writer. Television was still limited in its output and availability: most of the audience was watching sets in the windows of appliance stores. Remote controls were a long way off. It was the era of the great nightclubs that were the only place to see the super stars of the day, from Sinatra to Martin & Lewis. New York had The Copa, which was the top of the heap; Chicago had the Chez Paris; Miami, the Fontainebleau; L.A, the Coconut Grove; Atlanta, St. Louis, Milwaukee…every major city had one, and playing that circuit was the dream of every young comic.

That dream, however, usually started as a nightmare in hundreds of honky-tonk clubs affectionately known as "toilets", where the comics filled the time while the next stripper was getting dressed to get undressed. The audience was there to leer, not laugh, and if you managed to get off the stage in one piece, you were lucky. It was a gauntlet of bumps and bruises, but did offer young comics the luxury of learning their craft.

When Nietzsche said, "Whatever doesn't kill me makes me stronger," he hardly had comics in mind, but every night in joints all over America, more comics died than survived. Those who did survive took the next step to second-tier clubs where the comic was actually the attraction. The money was short, the pressure was great, and the management always was tough.

At the high end of this second tier was The Elegante on Ocean Parkway in Brooklyn. If you called any of the nightclubs in America at that time and asked for Rocco, the response would be, "Just a minute," or, "Speaking." At The Elegante, there was a *third* option: "Which one?"

A club with more than one Rocco was no place for the fainthearted, yet it was there that my partner, Sam Denoff, and I got our baptism by fire to the strange and wonderful world of writing comedy.

Sam and I had met while working at WNEW radio in New York. I had just left my $25 a week job for Cousin Lester, and Sam arrived two weeks later after a brief stint as "The Bargain Broadcaster" at Klein's Department store. If you were at Klein's in 1954, you might recall Sam's famous: "Attention shoppers! There is a truckload of half-priced Maidenform bras being delivered to the third floor." Sam got fired for adding: "This is a bust-out sale and I want to keep you abreast of it."

From the day Sam arrived, we became fast friends, and, over time, started writing comedy pieces for the station's disc jockeys. Our breakthrough came at the station's 1956 Christmas party where we performed a parody we had written about the station's management. It was funny enough to keep us from getting fired, but, more importantly, it got us George Shapiro, our first agent.

George had just been promoted from the William Morris mailroom, so we were also his first clients. We owe George more than any 10% commission could ever pay as do his later clients: Carl Reiner, Andy Kaufman, and Jerry Seinfeld.

George wasted no time getting us into the big time. In those days, the going rate for comedy material was $100 a minute. George demanded "$25 up front or not a word goes on paper."

Our first client was an unknown comic by the name of

Jimmy Casanova, whom we should have known would remain unknown when we suggested doing a routine on his name and he asked, "What's funny about Jimmy?" We ended up writing five minutes on moving the Dodgers to L.A. (including a song, "Let's keep the Dodgers in Brooklyn," later recorded by Phil Foster). We saw Jimmy perform the set once at a catering hall in Flatbush. It was awful, he was awful, and the food at the catering hall was awful. The only good thing was that he actually paid us the $500 by signing over a $600 insurance check covering an injury he sustained from a revolving door in Bloomingdale's. We had to give him cash for the $100 difference because he wouldn't take a check. Actually, as I think of it now, that's funnier than what we wrote.

Since it was the era of Martin & Lewis, every mediocre singer was teaming up with a marginally funny comedian in hopes of being the next Dean and Jerry. We went through most of them, including Stiles & Waring, Chase & Perry, Chase & Dean, Chase & Lester, Chase & Lenon. Finally, we convinced Chase that he was the problem and moved on to Lenon & Davis, Davis & Berlin, until finally Taylor & Mitchell and our introduction to Joe Scandori, who managed The Elegante.

Joe seemed too soft-spoken and decent for the rough and tumble nightclub world, which might explain the need for two Roccos. He also managed the hot-and-getting-hotter Don Rickles, so his interest in handling Taylor & Mitchell meant we were moving up in class. No more working for acts that appeared at weddings, bar mitzvahs, bars and conventions. Our comic genius would now be on display in a *real* club, with a stage and a band, for an audience of big spenders out on the town.

Well, almost, but not quite.

On weekend nights, The Elegante was the Brooklyn version of The Copa Cabana: plenty of action, and, if not the biggest stars, those on the way up or just starting down. Taylor & Mitchell were not yet in that class, so were relegated to performing midweek when The Elegante became a gathering place for some of the most bizarre audiences in show business history.

To keep the club operating fulltime, Joe created a package deal of dinner, dancing, and a show for $20 a person. It attracted groups and organizations for their special occasions, such as award ceremonies, installations of officers, or annual dances. The club was always sold out but to some pretty explosive combinations. On any given night at The Elegante, you would find the Canarsie B'nai B'rith seated next to the Red Hook Knights of Columbus, or the Bedford Stuyvesant NAACP shoulder to shoulder with the CTKBW (Committee To Keep Bay Ridge White). Since these groups came in thinking they would have the club to themselves, the night often started out as more of a meeting of mobs than an audience.

Joe handled the initial unrest by going on stage braced by the two Roccos, apologizing for the misunderstanding, and soothing it over with a round of free drinks. That prevented immediate bloodshed, and, because the food was good and plentiful, by show time the crowd's mood had elevated to surly. Getting this disparate group to actually become fun-loving for the acts to follow was the job of the emcee, Sal, who could have easily been the third Rocco. He was fearless and funny, attacking each group in turn until, gradually, they united in their hatred for Sal rather than each other and it was: "Show time!"

The opening act was a dance team featuring the suave Arturo and the seductive Lola (AKAs for Arnold Feingold and his cousin Laura). With Arturo's sexy smile, fancy footwork for the ladies, and daring lifts offering a fleeting glimpse of Lola's panties for the men, the tension eased and everyone actually started to have fun.

The second act was Rosemary DiTucci. Picture Rosemary Di Tucci: whatever your image, add 150 pounds, flaming red hair, and a voice that made Ethel Merman sound like the Singing Nun. She wowed them with show tunes, sing-alongs, and vulgar Italian ditties needing no translation.

After 20 minutes of Rosemary, the mood was set for the comedy to come. The stuff that worked best for the comics was down and, if not dirty, close to it. This wasn't the place for hip, topical, political, or subtle humor, which happened to be our best stuff.

For Taylor & Mitchell's first appearance at The Elegante, we wrote a breakthrough, clever, ripped-from-the-headlines routine about America's First Astronaut. Unfortunately, we were the only ones who read the headlines because none of the audience had any idea what an astronaut was, so Taylor & Mitchell never got off the ground.

As proof that the material was great, it was used three years later by Bill Dana in his platinum-selling Jose Jimenez album, *Jose the Astronaut*. But, on that night in 1957, we sat in a silent Elegante watching Taylor & Mitchell die…and thinking we were next.

The silence in Joe's office was even silenter as Taylor & Mitchell, Sam and me, the two Roccos and Sal waited for Joe to arrive. To make matters worse, the one window in the office overlooked a moonlit cemetery. It was like a scene from *The Godfather,* which was a dozen years away from being written. When Joe arrived, he walked methodically to his desk, sat, and looking more hurt than angry, slowly nodded his head. The Roccos joined in the nodding, followed by Sal, then Taylor & Mitchell. Not wanting to disagree with what appeared to be a unanimous conclusion, so did we.

Then Joe stopped nodding and we all stopped nodding.

A pause, then a raise of his eyes to Heaven followed by a riveting look at us and, in his soft, nice-guy voice, he said, "There didn't appear to be any laughter. Did anyone hear laughter?"

The Roccos and Sal were quick to agree, as were an unhappy Taylor & Mitchell, that, indeed, there had been no laughter.

We quickly pleaded guilty…with an explanation. We had written a great piece, but not for The Elegante, to which Joe, et al., agreed. We assured them that we had learned a valuable lesson and promised a whole new approach for the boys' next appearance and, obviously, there would be no charge.

"But there will be laughter," added Joe gently—leaving no doubt there'd *better* be.

And there was – lots of it – over the next months as we wrote for Taylor & Mitchell and some of the other acts Joe signed. We even wrote a funny speech for Rocco #1 to do at his daughter's wedding.

From there, with George selling and Joe giving us a thumbs-up to anyone checking us out, we moved to the top of the mountain: The Copa.

Marty "Hello dere" Allen and Steve Rossi, considered to be the next Martin & Lewis, were headlining and in search of new material. Every writer in town was fighting to get in, but they didn't have George Shapiro, and we did. After three years of working all day at WNEW, dining at the automat, and writing every night, we were actually sitting ringside at The Copa. We were "comped" as the guests of Allen & Rossi, whom we would meet after the show to discuss ideas. We were nervous but ready with a notebook full of really great stuff including a hilarious interview with President Eisenhower's caddie. They were going to love us!

The problem was we hated *them*. They were no Martin & Lewis. They weren't even Taylor & Mitchell. When they finished to a standing ovation I'll never understand, they headed toward us with an arrogant how-about-that swagger. We knew they were expecting praise, but even if it meant the end of our careers, we couldn't bring ourselves to offer it. Sam did manage a couple of noncommittal "Wow"s and "Man"s, which they took to mean he was awestruck. When they turned to me, I smiled and offered, "Boy, you guys sure fill 45 minutes," a simple statement of fact that their egos converted to acclaim.

Our meeting was a halfhearted affair since, as important as it could have been, we didn't want to write for them. Apparently, they were equally unimpressed with us, so it was back to The Elegante, but not for long. George was promoted to the television department at William Morris and moved to California with the promise he would have us there within a year.

He did it in six months, selling us as writers for *The Steve Allen Show*, the biggest variety show of the 1960 season. Steve had been the original host and creator of *The Tonight Show* and had gone on to do a groundbreaking variety show from New York in the late 50's. He moved to California for the new show and we were going with him, leaving The Elegante behind, but not the fun we'd had and the lessons we had learned.

A couple of things still make me smile when I think of The Elegante. There was no actual dressing room, just an area in the basement separated from the vegetable bins by a cyclone fence. Everyone—Arturo and Lola, Rosemary, the comics—shared the space. We would be there running lines with Taylor & Mitchell while Lola and Rosemary were dressing. It was understood that, as pros, we never looked at the "girls" while they were changing. That was no problem with Rosemary, but Lola was a knockout and it seems every guy from the kitchen showed up at the vegetable bins at those choice moments. From the smiles on their faces, I wish I had looked.

Also to this day, when I eat veal parmigiana, my thoughts are back at The Elegante. Not because it was the first place I ate it, but for how *often* I ate it. Once a week, for months, we would go to see Taylor & Mitchell and Joe would always greet us warmly and tell the waiter, "Give the boys whatever they want." We would always order steaks and lobster, but when the lights went down and the food was served, somehow it was veal parmigiana. About the tenth time, I actually ordered veal parmigiana to see what I'd get, and got veal parmigiana. On our last night at The Elegante, before leaving for L.A, we had already eaten so we didn't order anything. But when the lights went down, there it was on the table in front of us: veal parmigiana.

Those nights at The Elegante: of waiting for the laughs and the meetings to celebrate when they came—and sweat when they didn't—are part of everything that has happened to me since. After Joe, Sal, and the Roccos, there wasn't a network executive alive who seemed threatening, or an audience I didn't try to entertain and not show how clever I was. And there was never a performer I didn't live and die with when they were out there, trusting in me that "there would be laughter."

As it turned out, we would have just three weeks to make Steve Allen Laugh.

THE MOST IMPORTANT
JOKE I EVER WROTE

George had sold us as the hottest young writers in the business. To back it up, we sent Steve Allen a 10-pound package containing all the comedy material we had ever written. Steve was on tour and by the time the package arrived in L.A., he was in Texas; by the time it arrived there, he was in Chicago. That package followed him around the country for a month and he never actually got it, but with George on him every day, he finally took us on blind faith.

For the show, it was a small risk, but for Sam and me, it was like stepping off the edge of the planet: quitting our jobs and moving to California with a guarantee of only three weeks' work. If they liked us, we'd get three more, then another three, then three more, and then we'd be brought on for the full 26 shows. To make our decision even harder, the week we were leaving, we found out my wife was pregnant, but Sam and I knew this was our chance and we had to take it. In a sign you could read as good or bad, as we were leaving our apartment for the airport, the mailman came on his rounds and in his bag was our stamp-covered package, which had never been opened by Steve Allen, proving it is more important to have ten pounds of comedy material than for anyone to ever read it…and that George Shapiro was the best agent in the world.

It was an exciting and frightening time: living in a motel

until we knew if we could afford—or be around long enough—to need an apartment and going to work every day where we were surrounded by writers whose names we knew from the credits of big shows. The only other unknown was a guy we knew from New York, Buck Henry. Though everyone was supportive, it was like being on death row waiting for a reprieve. The first two weeks were nonproductive as we were learning our way around, and as the fatal third week started, we had done nothing to make us stand out. Things did not look good.

We were assigned to write the big sketch for the third show: clearly a test. It was a take-off on the major hit of the season, *Ben Casey*, the first big medical show, starring Vince Edwards as the earnest young doctor and Sam Jaffe as the wise old Dr. Zorba. Each week, the show opened with Dr. Zorba at a blackboard on which he chalked ancient symbols, and, in a wizened voice, made all the more serious with the hint of a Russian accent, he would, pointer in hand, explain them: "This is the sign for Man," then, moving down the list, "This is the sign for Woman; this is Birth; this is Death," and, at the very bottom, "and this is…Infinity."

We knew our lives were on the line as the Steve Allen cast – which now included a young comic from Cleveland, Tim Conway, and a comedy singing act, The Smothers Brothers – sat around the table for the script reading with Steve playing Ben Casey and Joey Forman, a great mimic, playing Dr. Zorba. Joey got a huge laugh on, "This is the sign for Man," just from his Zorba impression. He continued on: "This is Woman; this is Birth; this is Death; this is Infinity," and, instead of it ending there, at the bottom of the board, we had added the stick figure of a cat, "And this is a pussy cat."

Everyone exploded in laughter, Steve loudest and longest of all. He loved it and based on that one joke, we were picked up not just for three weeks, but for the whole season. Which was lucky because the show was cancelled after five weeks and they had to pay us for the whole 26, allowing us to stay in L.A.

THE *HARDEST* JOKE
I EVER WROTE

In 1962 we got a job writing a show for ABC to introduce the new fall lineup to affiliates at a meeting in Chicago. It was a full musical review with original songs, sketches, and monologues, featuring all the ABC stars which that year, included Gene Kelly who was in *Going My Way,* Gene Barry in *Burke's Law,* Chuck Connors in *The Rifleman,* Ozzie and Harriet and Jack Palance in *The Greatest Show on Earth.*

The performance was on Saturday afternoon with rehearsal the Friday before. Everyone was satisfied with the jokes we had written for them.

Everyone but film menace Jack Palance, who had just arrived after a 24-hour sleepless journey from Italy where he had just finished a film in which he had killed about a million people.

He was not in a good mood.

Since he was not famous for his sense of humor, we had written a nice, short speech about how he loved the circus and was thrilled to be doing the show. We were having a drink after the rehearsal when his agent came over to ask why Jack didn't have a joke. We explained that his show was a drama and that he was a serious actor, so a joke didn't seem right.

The agent returned ten minutes later with these chilling words: "Jack wants a joke. Come to his room and write one."

Jack Palance was frightening under any circumstances,

but grouchy from no sleep after killing a million people—he was terrifying. After about a hundred jokes, none of which elicited the slightest indication of amusing him, he was starting to become annoyed. Picture being trapped in a room with him when he was unhappy.

Finally, Sam said something and Jack intoned "Haargh," a kind of a snarl, as if he was about to attack.

"He likes it," translated his agent as Jack let out another "Haargh." Given that there is no guarantee that any joke will work and concerned that if he didn't get a laugh at the show he might come after us, we told him we were going to give him a "saver." Looking much like his ice-blooded gunfighter character from *Shane*, he asked why the joke wouldn't get a laugh.

We assured him it would, but just in case, the saver definitely would: "If you want to see *The Greatest Show on Earth*, just watch what I do to the guys who told me that was funny."

We got a "Haargh, haargh," and escaped to the bar. I'm sure you would like to know the joke, but frankly, I don't remember it. I do remember it got a huge laugh—probably because no one expected Jack Palance to tell a joke.

He was stunned and when the laughter died down he said, "If you want to see *The Greatest Show on Earth*, watch what I do to the guys who told me that was funny," at which point the audience was also stunned, and he walked off the stage in a daze. We heard he was looking for us later, and since we weren't sure why, we hid in our room.

THE WISDOM OF
JERRY GRANT

You're just going to have to take my word for it when I tell you about Jerry Grant because he seems like a character made up by Damon Runyon, Jimmy Breslin, or Pete Hamill: three of the greatest New York storytellers of all time. Actually, it would have taken all three to come up with Jerry.

Jerry Grant was the up and downside of every New York guy of fact and fiction: a Yankee fan who could beat a computer head-to-head on statistics and do a play-by-play rebroadcast of every important game the Yankees ever played. He was funnier than Jackie Gleason, Alan King and Jerry Lewis, all of whom he wrote for, and he knew more about music than Sinatra, Tony Bennett, and Dean Martin, who were his pals.

He was also the most devious person I have ever known, but my life is better for his having been in it.

We met in 1961 when I was 30 and he was in his 60s. Sam and I had been hired as junior writers on *The Andy Williams Show* where Jerry was the old pro under Head Writer "Velvet" Len Golde: Velvet, not for his smooth manner, but his suit jackets and sport coats, which all had velvet collars, most of them frayed since he had been out of work for a while.

Jerry and Len were like Godzilla meets King Kong, so Sam and I just tried not to get killed by the falling rubble. Comedy writers had two evaluations of one another: you were either a wonderful guy who couldn't write his name, let alone a joke; or the funniest guy in the world, but don't turn your back on him. Jerry was the funny-don't-turn-your-back variety, while Len was unique—you couldn't turn your back on him *and* he couldn't write his name, let alone a joke.

Len was also no match for Jerry, who had an amazing ability to take credit for everything that went right, and no part of what went wrong. It was fascinating to watch him in action. When something got a big laugh, he muttered to no one in particular, but audible to all: "I told you! Didn't I tell you?" If it failed, there was a dismissive "Huh? What did I say? What did I say?" But his greatest move was when Andy particularly liked something and he'd offer: "I thought you'd like that."

The maddening thing was that he didn't blatantly take credit, so you couldn't challenge him, and, yet, by letting it go by, it seemed as if he had done it all. I watched in amazement as he manipulated his way in, and Len's out. Then it was our turn.

Though he liked us, it was just his nature not to give ground, and he did enough to keep us in our place. During the Len/Jerry struggle, we were doing most of the writing with no recognition except for Jerry's "The boys are okay," when asked for an evaluation. For that, he assumed he had earned our unquestioned loyalty.

Once Len was gone, we were a well-oiled machine: us writing and Jerry taking the credit. Then, during a script reading, with the entire crew, network executives, and people from the ad agency assembled, he made a move worthy of Machiavelli. As Andy read his opening monologue, there was a joke that got a huge laugh, and when the laughing subsided, Jerry got everyone's attention to announce: "The boys wrote that!"

We were thrilled at the recognition and I remember thinking we had had Jerry all wrong. Then, page after page, laugh after laugh, all on jokes we had written, he never said it again, clearly creating the impression that the rest were all his. It was masterful, and though you had to hate him, you couldn't help but love him for the rogue he was.

The sad thing is that he really *was* brilliantly funny! He just never trusted himself, or anyone else for that matter, so his every minute was dedicated to self-preservation. It's hard to believe you could learn something of value from someone so devoid of principles, but on Thanksgiving in 1961, he passed on one of "Grant's Laws" which has served me well a thousand times since.

My wife planned a very formal dinner for ten and ordered elegant china, silverware, glasses, and linens from Abbey Rents, the top-of-the-line caterer in L.A. When I got home on Wednesday night, the table was set perfectly...except for one detail.

As I'd been leaving work, Dave Grusin, Andy's musical director, found himself alone for Thanksgiving because his wife had been called out of town. I invited him to join us, thinking a friend shouldn't be alone, but giving no thought that one place setting at my wife's table wouldn't match.

She made it abundantly and repeatedly clear that she didn't see things the same way. Since I wasn't about to uninvite Dave, and knew there would be nothing to be thankful for if I didn't solve the problem, I called Abbey Rents to get another setting delivered. They were closed for the night and on Thanksgiving Day as well, but with a little pleading I arranged to have someone be there so that I could come by at noon to pick it up, thus managing to save the day.

The complication was that we were working Thanksgiving Day and there wasn't a free minute as we pushed to get home for dinner, so getting to Abbey Rents at noon was out of the question. It was obvious to everyone with whom I worked that my wife should just go pick up the place setting, but only because they didn't know her: *I* had caused the problem, ergo *I* had to fix it. As I worked my typewriter with one hand and the phone with the other to arrange a later pickup, Jerry took the phone from my hand, hung it up, and just like The Gambler in the Kenny Rodgers song, "gave me an ace that I could hold." It was right out of his deck stacked for self-preservation and taking care of Number One.

"Billy, hang on every word," which was his standard introduction when he was offering something profound. He asked if I knew what life insurance was and I assured him I did—insurance you have on your life to provide for your loved ones when you die.

"No," he said, "that is *death* insurance. *Life* insurance is for you to make sure you don't die *before* you have to, by being very good to yourself." He went on to explain that I was going to call a messenger to pick up at Abbey Rents while I ordered some lunch and had some fun with the guys writing the show. The messenger was going to cost about $20, which I was to consider my first insurance premium.

It seemed so obvious, but so easy to miss, so, thanks to Jerry, I took out my policy that day and it has saved me, if not my life, certainly a lot of stress, time, and aggravation.

I set a limit for any one-time premium at $100 and I figure that in the past 30 years this life insurance has cost me a few thousand dollars: calling messengers to pick up or deliver when it made life easier; not fighting with service people who didn't provide the service they were paid for; not returning things I had bought that didn't work if the store was too far away; not haggling the price on things I really wanted; skipping the theater on a really miserable night even though I had tickets; plus dozens of other meaningless things that might not have preserved my life but have certainly enhanced it.

THE WORST NIGHT
OF MY LIFE

It turns out, what I really needed insurance from was Jerry Grant himself.

He struck right before the wrap party to celebrate the last Andy Williams show of the season. We were called into the producer's office and told we were not coming back for season two. Jerry, in his Machiavellian way, had managed to take credit for all we had done and didn't want us around now that we were getting wise to him. He went into great detail about how he had fought for us and, to prove how good a manipulator he was, we actually believed him.

We didn't much feel like going to the party, but figured we couldn't just slink into the night in disgrace, so we walked in with forced smiles and a "That's show business!" bravado, which didn't work for us or anyone else. It was a disaster; everyone knew and you could feel everyone wishing us gone.

The only person who came over to say how sorry she felt was Andy's wife, Claudine Longet, an act of kindness that had me convinced of her innocence two years later when she allegedly shot and killed her ski instructor-boyfriend.

As we drove through pouring rain in my rented convertible that I knew I would have to turn in for something out-of-work writers drive, the mood inside the car was as depressing as the weather outside. All we wanted to do was go some place to drink and brood, but we had already made plans to meet a comedy team about writing their act. They were working the lounge at the Covina Bowling Alley—hardly the road to Vegas— but now that we were out of television, a hundred dollars a minute sounded pretty good. When we arrived at the Covina Bowl, it was league night, so the lot was packed and we had to park about a block away. Because no one in California owns an umbrella, by the time we met the comics we were soaked and the air conditioning in the bowling alley was at sub-zero.

As the big attraction for hiring us had been our job on *The Andy Williams Show*, we left out the fact we'd been fired, covering it with a false gaiety verging on hysteria. They were overly cocky and hysterical themselves—to make up for the fact they were working in a bowling alley.

The jokes were flying, the laughter forced, as we tried to look like anything but what we were: the four biggest losers in show business. We didn't end up writing for them, and couldn't even tell if they were funny because every time they got to a punch line, someone would bowl a strike and the cheering drowned them out.

We drove home in silence through the rain, wondering if things would ever be good again. They got better than ever when George went into action and got us a chance to work on *The Dick Van Dyke Show*, the most sought-after job in television.

By the way, the comics we met at the bowling alley were Rowan and Martin, and things didn't go badly for them afterward either.

ONLY IN HOLLYWOOD

Levita Levanthal could have been the symbol of America if they hadn't decided on the eagle. She was feistier, nobler, prouder, and just as dangerous. Her family had come to Arizona by covered wagon in the late 1800s to fight the last of the Indians, the desert, and anything else standing in the way of building a ranch. From the stories she told, John Wayne wouldn't have been tough enough to play her father, and when she came into my life in 1962 at the age of 75, it would have taken Kathy Bates with a touch of Clint Eastwood to play her.

In a life story too involved to re-tell here (trust me—it's epic), which would read like a testament to the pioneer spirit, the only unlikely chapter was being housekeeper to a Jewish couple with a newborn baby in the Hollywood of the 60s. There was nothing that went on in the world, and very little in our home, she approved of, but with it all there was a gentle goodness that made her a treasure. She had rockbound rules for everything, especially child-rearing, and I can only apologize to Dana for some of them and be grateful that others were there to guide us. It was kind of like living with General Patton if he could bake the best pies ever baked. Nothing impressed her about "that show business," which made the events of Christmas Eve 1963 all the more special.

We were going to Danny Thomas' Christmas Eve party which brought together every great comedian you could think of, leaving Levi watching *White Christmas*, one of the few movies of which she approved, and Bing Crosby, who, according to her was the only true movie star. She was shocked and disbelieving when I told her Irving Berlin, who wrote White Christmas, was Jewish, and struck dumb that he had also written "God Bless America." In the end, she accepted it with her basic credo about everything: "Well, there you go, don't you? People are just people." When we left that evening, she was sitting in her favorite chair with a smile on her face, Bing Crosby singing just for her.

When we returned four hours later, she was still sitting in her favorite chair with a smile still on her face with the television still on. She showed no sign of life as we came in and I was sure she was dead as I approached her tentatively, not wanting to frighten her if she wasn't…or me if she was. Gradually, she responded to our presence, but was still in some kind of trance. I said her name softly and her smile widened. "Are you all right?" I asked. With a wider smile and a gentle head shake, she added, "He was *here*…" with such a sense of reverence I thought she had had a vision of the baby Jesus himself.

Cautiously I asked, "Who was here?'

Still not quite back in the real world, she said, "Bing."

I repeated. "Bing?"

She clarified: "Bing Crosby."

Assuming she had fallen asleep during the movie and had had a dream, I offered, "Oh, on the *TV!*" She, very defensively: "No, not on the TV! *Here!*" Still not sure how to handle whatever was going, I went along: "Oh, Bing Crosby was here," immediately thinking it was time to look for a new housekeeper.

In her full Levi Levanthal attack mode: "Don't patronize me! When I say 'Bing Crosby was *here*,' you'd better *believe he was here!*" And she handed me a piece of paper she had been clutching on which was written:

> *To Levi,*
> *Thanks and have a Merry Christmas.*
> *Bing Crosby*

Obviously, unless she was into spirit writing, Bing Crosby had been there! In a set of circumstances that could only have taken place before the advent of cell phones, while she had been watching *White Christmas,* the doorbell rang, and when she'd asked, "Who's there?" she heard, "It's Bing Crosby," who, at that moment, was singing on her television set. She challenged, and he responded that it was actually he. She put the chain on the door and opened it to find that it was, in fact, actually Bing Cosby.

He had gotten a flat tire on his way up the hill to a party and wanted to call for someone to pick him up. As he waited, they watched the movie together and he told her some behind-the-scenes stories.

His ride arrived and as he was leaving, he thanked her, gave her the autograph, and she, in a most un-Levi like moment, asked him to sing "White Christmas" for her, which he did, leaving her in the happy state in which we'd found her.

THE GIFT OF
CARL REINER

Working with Carl Reiner was the best thing (after the birth of my children and my marriage to Joanna) that ever happened to me. He was already a legendary comedian from his years as a writer and performer with Sid Caesar on the revered 50s comedy classic, *Your Show of Shows*. Carl moved into the top ranks of writer-producer-director of the award-winning *Dick Van Dyke Show*. These days, in his late eighties, he keeps right on going as George Clooney's right-hand man in the *Oceans* movies, along with guest appearances on every comedy show that needs a brilliant older guy…or some help with the writing.

In 1963, *The Dick Van Dyke Show* was starting its third season and was already considered the high point in the development of situation comedy. Every writer in Hollywood was writing a sample script trying to get Carl's attention, but ours had a little something extra: George, who just happened to be Estelle Reiner's nephew. But, when it comes to writing comedy, nepotism will get you only so far.

Though our script was flawed, Carl liked the writing so much that he gave us an assignment to do a show, and everything really good in my career started at that moment. Carl would be my mentor, my hero, my role model and for the next 50 years, my friend. Everything I write, and much of how I live my life, is a reflection of his integrity, fairness, decency, and, yes, his fearlessness.

THAT'S MY BOY!

That was the title of the first *Van Dyke* of the 45 we wrote. It was a flashback episode about the birth of Richie, The Petrie's son, based on the premise that Dick (playing suburbia-dwelling TV writer Rob Petrie), through a series of circumstances, thinks the baby they brought home is not theirs but that of another couple—the Peters—with whom they had been regularly confused at the hospital: the wrong flowers, the wrong dinner...

The story was perfect for Dick to play, but there was one problem; since this was prior to the introduction of DNA, there was no irrefutable way to prove the baby was actually the Peters' baby, except by either another nationality or color. This was 1963 and racial issues were at a highly volatile point in this country, so Carl decided we'd hit on a perfect time to lighten the mood. We made the Peters black.

At the very end of the show, Rob insists the Peters come over with their baby, which Rob is absolutely convinced is his, and make the switch. When the doorbell rings, he very resolutely steps up to the door, assuring his wife, Laura (Mary Tyler Moore), despite her violent protestations, that he knows what he's doing.

"Laura, I think it would be best if you went to your room. I will handle this." He opens the door and is stunned to see Mr. Peters, played by Greg Morris (of *Mission Impossible* fame).

When the script went to the network, the censors immediately called in panic and said it was not acceptable. Carl asked why, and they said it was obvious, to which Carl responded, "Not to me."

A flurry of calls followed with neither side giving in, and Carl was called to the network where all kinds of executives assembled to give him a group "No!" Which didn't stop him. He wanted them to tell him why not and not just assume he should know. Carl acknowledged race was a touchy area, which, as far as he was concerned, made it time for someone to touch it.

The executives all agreed—except that the "touching" should not be done at that moment by that network. "The country is not ready for a white couple to make a black couple the butt of a joke."

Carl assured them that wasn't the case; it was the black couple that was making the white couple the butt of the joke, to which the executives responded:

"The country certainly isn't ready for *that!*"

Still, Carl refused to give in and somehow (I think going to the press was mentioned) he finally won the argument.

The Dick Van Dyke Show was filmed in front of a live audience and all during rehearsals there was an air of anxiety: What would actually happen when Mr. Peters, played by Greg Morris, walked through the door?

When the climactic moment came I was standing next to Carl and when Greg appeared in the doorway, there was total silence from the audience of 300 people: a silence long enough for Carl to whisper, "Oh, shit!"

Then there came an explosive laugh that lasted for literally 20 minutes, which lasted just 15 seconds in the edited version. Every time we tried to start the scene again, the laughter would start anew. On the night of September 16, 1963, television history was made and a major step taken in the treatment of African Americans on television, and Carl had lightened the mood…just as he had hoped.

***

Not all of Carl's fearlessness was expressed in such important matters. More often than not, it was just in the day-to-day puncturing of pompous people's balloons no matter what their status or the consequences. At the start of the fourth season of the show, CBS appointed a tough new Head of Programming. He came out from New York, going from show to show to let people know he was in charge and there were tough times ahead. He had everyone scared to death…until he came to the *Van Dyke* show.

His first mistake was putting his feet on the coffee table.

Carl let that go by.

His second misstep was his arrogant declaration of how things were going to be run from now on.

Carl let that one go by, too.

His third was to pontificate on his theory of comedy and what was funny. Carl didn't let that go by: He got up from his desk, walked across the room, pulled off the man's Gucci loafer and threw it out the window, stating, "Now, that's funny."

After a silence—at least as long as the one when Greg Morris walked through Rob Petrie's door, the guy started to laugh and we never had a problem with him again.

Carl did not suffer fools; he just couldn't sit by and let people say or do stupid things without calling them on it. I had been the victim of those call-outs on a number of occasions, and, as uncomfortable as they might have been, they were always a learning experience.

One classic Carl moment was during a meeting with a very "natty" comedy writer who was always dressed in up-to-the-minute style, and whose vanity included a comb-over of his three six-foot long strands of remaining hair, a procedure that must have taken hours every day as he laced the strands back and forth. The strands fooled nobody, looking more like the strings on a zither than a head of hair. The man had been doing the comb-over for years and though everyone made jokes about it, no one ever said anything. Until Carl.

All through the meeting, Carl couldn't take his eyes off the guy's hair, and finally said, "Leon, you're bald." Everyone's focus went to Leon's strands. "You know it, everyone knows it, and it's hard to take you seriously with this thing on your head." At which point Carl took the end of the strands and walked six feet until he and Leon's head looked like the supporting poles of a tightrope. Even for Carl, this was pushing it, until Leon, looking at the absurdity of Carl standing six feet away holding his hair, started to laugh, finally realizing in that moment how ridiculous it was. He cut off the hair and bought a toupee, which *also* looked ridiculous but at least was an admission that the man was bald.

Carl did have a thing about hair and I personally have been the recipient of two Carl Reiner haircuts, as well as one eyebrow trimming.

CONAN THE
BARBARIAN & ME

Carl once said he didn't believe Englishmen really had accents; they just all got together and agreed to talk that way in order to make the rest of us feel bad. The tendency was probably rooted in feelings of inadequacy dating back to their origins as Druids who were still running around painted blue long after everyone else had moved on to cooked food and world conquest. Carl believed the accents were all for effect, and that if, at three in the morning, you crept into a room where an Englishman was sleeping and shouted "Fire!" he would wake in panic and say "Fire? Let's get the hell outta here!" with no accent whatsoever, sounding very much like the rest of us.

Though I would gladly lose my New York accent under any circumstance, I have beliefs, values, and images of myself I would like to think are real. I couldn't help but wonder how they would hold up if Carl crept into my room some night and sounded the alarm.

I know who I would *like* to be in that rude awakening— grabbing the kids and the cat and leading everyone in the building to safety in a calm, clear voice that I must admit, I have already selected from several I have tried out in the shower. It is the one I have when I am working and sure of myself. It is also the one I try to recreate when I am threatened and unsure, hoping the hollowness I hear in my ears and feel in my soul isn't being conveyed.

But I have always known that if that moment came, no matter what I had hoped or planned, there are no accents or images—there is only *you*, the *real* you, the one you doubt, question, and hide from the world and with less success, from yourself.

My moment came one summer morning in the early 90s. It wasn't 3 a.m., but sometime after 5, and it wasn't Carl Reiner shouting, "Fire!" but a muffled thumping sound made by a man climbing through my bedroom window. Instantly, I found out who I was: the unlikely combination of Arnold Schwarzenegger and my mother…and I'm still not sure who was the more effective.

I leapt naked from my bed, grabbed the first weapon at hand—my Ralph Lauren pillow—and went on the attack screaming "Get out! Get out!" in a high-pitched voice. I resented my mother speaking for me at a time like that and consciously tried to get into a lower register, one that had more indignation than fear, but it was her moment and I couldn't take it away from her.

The Schwarzenegger part of the equation was doing a lot better, and I was pleased with him actually forging into battle: hand-to-hand combat with the intruder who was three-quarters of the way into the room. The window only opened a foot and a half, held in place by a dowel I had inserted between the top and the frame to prevent anyone from climbing in. I made a note to get a longer pole if I lived.

The struggle raged as my burglar—we'd known each other long enough at this point for some familiarity—was pushing against a flower box to come the rest of the way in as I was pushing and swinging my pillow to get him out.

I needed a more formidable weapon. It was right there on the night table, but in my initial panic I had missed it: Tom Wolfe's three-pound novel, *The Bonfire of the Vanities*. Hitting the intruder with that would have done major damage and in a perverse way, have been some kind of social comment. But there I was, a death grip on my Ralph Lauren pillow, flailing and shrieking in stark terror and stark nakedness, which also didn't help my cause. With the possible exception of the nude wrestling scene from *Women in Love*, no man would choose to go into battle in that condition. I'm sure there are deep psychological reasons, but the more immediate ones are one's acute vulnerability and the embarrassing thought of being found *that* way in the morning.

New York Post headlines flashed through my mind.

We were at a stalemate given that the narrow opening was preventing either of us from making any headway. My warrior self, with Zen clarity, suddenly perceived that if I removed the pole, I could open the window fully and my chances of getting him all the way out would improve. The thought that my moving the pole would improve *his* chance of getting all the way *in* hadn't occurred to me. That's the trouble with Zen: it's so self-involved.

I emitted a fierce yell I had borrowed from a sushi chef in Malibu, and yanked the pole free. Suddenly the tide of battle turned in my favor as he was now up against a naked maniac with a pole instead of a pillow, and my mother switched from "Get out! Get out!" to a more macho, "You son-of-a-bitch!"

The combination must have been awesome because he started to plead in what I am sure was *his* mother's voice: "Don't hurt me! Don't hurt me!"

Don't hurt *him?* The thought never entered my mind, but as long as he brought it up as an option, I considered it. I could use the new upper body strength I'd developed at the Vertical Club to knock him senseless. I had originally planned on using this strength to improve my tennis serve, but now the strength seemed to serve a higher purpose: not just complaining about street crime, but stopping it single-handedly. The *Post* headlines were improving.

The struggle intensified until somehow his mother and my mother got to talking—as mothers will—and, "Don't hurt me! Don't hurt me!" seemed like a good idea all around. So I gave him a shove that wasn't needed to get him out and covered his escape up a tree and over a wall with a hail of four-letter words, finally finding the voice I had planned on for the occasion.

I closed and locked the window and drew the draperies (funny how the minute the problem is over we do all the things that would have prevented the event in the first place). I stood waiting. I wasn't sure for what, probably to go into shock or some other reaction that comes when danger is past.

What came was a sense of...*power!*

This was only the second real fight I'd ever had. The first had been in the third grade when Jerry Matz challenged me to meet him after school for reasons I can't for the life of me recall, but I think it was about who was going to marry Nina Yanoff. What I do remember is that I was nauseous all day and cried throughout the fight, even after I had won. Now, here I was, not crying, not even breathing hard. I settled for calling the police. I considered not bothering because the incident was over, but I felt it was the responsible thing to do. Besides, I was dying to tell somebody.

I filed a report and now my burglar and I are just another crime statistic-- along with the other apartment on 62nd Street that was burglarized that night while the occupants slept. The police are sure it was my burglar after he left me, so apparently our encounter had had very little impact on the direction of his life. But it did have a very profound effect on mine.

I made the obvious adjustments of sleeping in shorts, keeping the fireplace poker next to my bed, and getting bars for the windows. That information is for my burglar—in case he is thinking of coming back.

On another obvious level, the incident made me contemplate the fleeting nature of life and living every moment since because the police assured me that if he had been armed or out of control on drugs, the *Post* would have indeed had its headline.

On a less obvious but more meaningful level is how I see myself in Carl Reiner's hypothesis. Who I am at the core? Tougher and braver than I knew, even with the high-pitched voice (my policeman said he wouldn't have been able to speak at all). I really like the guy who I turned out to be. I'd like to be that guy more often, and I think I know why I'm not.

It isn't a question of courage, but of clarity, and the freedom that comes when you know you're right. In our daily lives, it's never as obvious as someone coming through our bedroom window. It's vague or obtuse, and our first instinct waits as we filter through too much information and conditioning, and we lose that first impulse, which is pure *us*.

My burglar probably had a lousy childhood; he might be a terrific kid with all kinds of potential who never had a chance. In retrospect, he might be the real victim. But that night he was coming through my bedroom window and one thing was crystal clear—he didn't belong there. So I was free to act as who I really am.

It was a great feeling, one I would like to hold on to, trust, and go with. Every day there are less obvious intruders coming through the windows of my spirit and my soul, and they don't belong there either.

Let them beware! Arnold and my mother are waiting.

STARS AREN'T
LIKE US

Today the word "Star" is used for everyone from the dysfunctional Housewives of Everywhere to the dancing unwed daughter of Sarah Palin, but there was a time—a better time— when it meant something more.

A Star was someone we looked up to, not down on. A Star shone and lit the way, filling us with wonder as something to admire and aspire to, not smirk at. Stars were special people, and were Stars before they—or we—knew it. They are just different from us, and when you see it you know it.

In 1965, Sam and I were casting *Good Morning World*, a show about two disk jockeys based on the start of our career at WNEW radio.

We were looking for the wife of the lead, and, having just finished *The Dick Van Dyke Show*, like everyone else we were looking for the next Mary Tyler Moore—a search that goes on to this day because there was and will always be, only one. We were about to interview the 15th and final actress of the day, and the minute she came in, we knew she was wrong for the part: cute, sexy, but not beautiful; quirky and childlike, not wife-like. Yet there was something special about her.

This was her first acting audition and she was so excited—her only previous experience having been as a dancer on TV variety shows. The scene called for the wife to be pouring tea and she had brought her own teapot as a prop. We were hoping she would prove us wrong. As she read, it was clear she wasn't right for the part, but even clearer that she was a Star—you just *knew*. I looked at Sam and could tell he agreed.

When she was finished, after telling her she wasn't right for the wife, I told her she was perfect for the part of the wife's best friend. She said that when she had read the script there was no best friend and I said, "That was before you came in."

That was Goldie Hawn's first job as an actress, and where George Schlatter found her for Rowan & Martin's *Laugh-In*.

A couple of years later when casting another series, an actress who had been in L.A for only a week came in to audition for a small part that she could have had the minute she walked through the door. She was beautiful, sexy, charming, and from the reading, clearly a good actress. I told her she could have the part, and after her celebration, added that she shouldn't take it: explaining it wasn't good enough for her. She still wanted it and I told her it was hers, but she should think it over. Trust me, I told her, this part would tie her up, holding her back from much bigger things.

She trusted me and three weeks later she was one of Charlie's Angels.

FARRAH

For her, one name will always be enough.

Though she died in a most unglamorous fashion, she is still remembered for her golden mane and killer smile. In the 80s, as Charlie's highest flying Angel, she was a role model for teenage girls, and a fantasy for boys of *all* ages. But even more than the show, it was the red bathing suit poster that made her an icon of the decade.

That image was everywhere: in school lockers, on the walls of service stations, dorm rooms, and countless prison cells. It was a simple enough poster, just her with a smile that said whatever you wanted it to, kneeling on her haunches, wearing what would've been without her in it, a rather ordinary red bathing suit. The combination of her and the suit was devastating.

My twin daughters, Jamie and Liza, who were 11, each had one of those posters over their beds.* They adored her, although Liza also had a strong commitment to Lindsey Wagner, the Bionic Woman, which I think was the result of Jamie claiming Farrah first.

Jamie constantly carried a cigar box containing 2,000 pictures of Farrah (with no duplications) wherever she went, including the day she met her. We were spending Saturday afternoon, as we often did, at the Laughlins – Dodie and Tom, of the *Billy Jack* films.

It was always open house at the Laughlins with tennis, swimming, then dinner and a movie. You never knew who would show up to join the regulars: Carl Reiner and family, Mel Brooks and Anne Bancroft, Tim Conway, Harvey Korman, Tim Van Patten and family who, on this particular day, brought their good friend, Farrah Fawcett.

Farrah gave me a hug, and I introduced her to the girls, which enshrined me as a Hero For Life in their eyes and put them into a state of ecstasy and shock. After kissing me on the cheek where she had, they honed in and never let her out of sight, the cigar box clutched tightly in Jamie's hand.

They knew not to intrude on her privacy and kept their distance, but every time Farrah turned around, there they were until finally she walked over to talk to them. Before she even got there, Jamie exploded, "I have 2,000 pictures of you in this box!"

Obviously impressed, Farrah responded: "Two thousand?"

Liza quickly added, "And no duplicates."

"Well," she said, "that's quite a collection. Maybe I should take a look."

And for the next hour, with Jamie and Liza seated adoringly beside her, Farrah went through the pictures, telling inside stories about some of them. If they were fans before, they were fanatics from then on, and if Farrah ever needed a body part for a transplant, they would have been willing donors.

When we were leaving, I thanked Farrah and suggested she join the Van Pattens who were coming to our house in Malibu the next day for lunch. When I told the girls she was coming, they gulped in a huge breath, which they didn't let out until she actually arrived Sunday afternoon.

It was a beautiful day and we all decided to go for a swim before lunch, and as if the girls weren't thrilled enough that she was there, Farrah came down to the beach wearing *it:* the red bathing suit, which looked even better in person.

Not only were the kids dazzled, but within minutes the word spread that *she* was there, and by the time we came out of the water, there were dozens of people waiting to greet Farrah. She graciously posed for pictures and signed autographs as we made our way through the mob.

Back at the house, she took a shower and left the red bathing suit hanging in the bathroom to dry. When the word got out that it was in there, unguarded, the temptation was too great for Jamie and Liza and I only regret I don't have any pictures of the magic moment when they tried it on. Although there have been many magical moments in their lives, I'm sure nothing will ever top it, especially now that the suit is in The Smithsonian.

*I wouldn't embarrass Liza with this if she hadn't already been exposed to the world on *The Rosie O'Donnell Show,* which she produced. She was thrilled when Farrah was booked as a guest, and ecstatic when she was assigned to handle Farrah's appearance because she knew more about Farrah than Farrah herself. For some reason, of all the fan crushes she had had over the years, Farrah outlasted them all, as had her collection of Farrah "stuff": dolls, a lunchbox, backpack , t-shirt, coloring book, a weird shadow box with 12 Farrah doll heads, and—every 11-year-old's dream—a pair of Farrah Fawcett underpants. Liza was encouraged to bring it all as part of the segment so Rosie could set up a mini Farrah museum. Out of respect, Liza left out the underpants, which, for the fun of it, she decided to wear. The high point of the day was that Farrah remembered Liza and they talked about what fans she and Jamie had been. Liza, caught up in the moment, told her about the underpants, which led to the low point when Farrah told Rosie. Suddenly the camera was on Liza who, ready to die, had to lower the top of her jeans just enough to show Farrah's smiling face.

DANJALI*

*I don't know if it's in the Old Testament, or just an understood 11th commandment, but it is incumbent upon Jewish people to christen things with a combination of their children's names. Don Rickles observed that only the Israeli Navy has a battleship called *The Mindybeth*.

Also, there is a high rate of emotional problems in those born *after* the family business—or the boat—has been named for their preceding siblings. Not wanting to take any chances with my three daughters—Dana, Jamie, and Liza—Danjali was the name of my production company, and *Jalida*, my boat.

It's a given that we love our children. It comes with the territory. They're born, we love them; they grow, we love them; do good, love them; bad, love them; do nothing and we love them for that, too. But, if you're lucky, there's another level; not a given but a gift. It comes out of nowhere and happens in a moment, a moment you don't expect, but when you see it, you know, because at that moment you get to fall in love with your child. And that doesn't come with the territory.

I've been fortunate to have that moment with each of my three daughters, and though the circumstances differed, in each case I had a glimpse of who they were deep within, an essence that was purely them. I got to see their souls, and after that, all the rules changed.

There is an emotional bank account to draw on when circumstances and events might otherwise deplete your patience, understanding and commitment. In recalling these events, I am leaving out references to their mother not to imply a lack of involvement, but because these are my personal remembrances and the effect they had on me.

My eldest is Dana, whose countless achievements and virtues are less her measure than the obstacles she climbed over, under, and through to become the person she is today. It was a difficult journey, and, en route, we faltered and sometimes lost our way. I say *we*, because from the age of 12, I reared her by myself. The circumstances of the separation from her mother are not important here, nor are blame, fault, or cause. It's enough to say it was not a happy time, and any 12-year-old girl would have found it difficult as would any 43-year-old single father trying to raise her, and, in many ways, himself (see "Come on Maidenhair Fern" later). I'm sure we made it through all the pitfalls because, in my heart, I knew under it all Dana was the pure, gentle essence I fell in love with one day in 1965 when she was three.

We were at a golf tournament sponsored by "The Wood Hackers," a catch-all group of actors, writers, and show people in general who shared the belief that lousy golf is best played in the company of heavy drinking, fun-loving companions amid lavish surroundings. There was a tournament every two months in Palm Springs, Pebble Beach, or some other great place. The events always tied to a local charity, and we'd put on a great show to raise a lot of money while raising a lot of hell. This particular match was at Torrey Pines, a resort outside of San Diego on a cliff overlooking the Pacific.

We had never taken Dana to any of "The Hacker" events because they weren't really meant for children, but this one was different. Billy Barty, the wonderful "little person," had just become a "Hacker" and was going to be there. He and Dana had fallen in love when she had met him on the set of one of my shows where he was playing an elf. Once she heard Billy would be at the tournament, she just couldn't be denied. In the days leading up to the tourney, she asked every 10 minutes if it was time yet, and tried on every dress she owned, selecting her "princess one"—a pink party dress—to be accessorized with a pink barrette and black shoes set off by white, lace-topped socks. Writing this description here, I see her clearly before me.

As the only kid at the weekend, she became the darling of all and, bless Billy, he didn't shirk his role as new best friend. She followed him everywhere and because they were about the same size, they actually looked like a couple. To top it off, he taught her a little dance step to do with him in the show. By the time Sunday arrived, Dana had left Cloud Nine for Cloud Ten. The dinner and show were scheduled for 6 p.m. and she was dressed and ready at noon. Even a chance to go in the pool couldn't get her to change her wardrobe, which she had kept spot-free through lunch and countless snacks. It was a day she would never forget even before it took a turn that left her with a constant reminder.

We had gone to our room to get ready for the party and took a moment on the deck for the last few breathtaking moments of the sun sliding into the Pacific. There was a strong breeze coming off the water and you could almost smell Hawaii in the distance. Dana had time for none of it as she sat, cross-legged at the door, ready to go. I thought I heard someone knock, and since she was closest, asked her to see who it was. I heard the door open and the wind swept past me in the draft created by the opening. In the next instant there was the harsh crash of the door slamming shut and a terrifying scream.

I turned to see the door had closed on her hand. Her cries

combined pain, disbelief, and terror. What had happened? What would happen? I was afraid opening the door might inflict new damage, but clearly I couldn't leave things as they were.

In one swift move I yanked it, freeing her. As she fell to the ground, I told my wife to get the car as I carried Dana to the bathroom to wash away the blood and assess the damage. Amazingly, in the midst of it all, she fought to keep the princess dress safe. Everything else was saturated and, clearly, I had to get her to a hospital. I grabbed a towel and, on the way down the hall, grabbed a bucket of ice from a room service cart and wrapped her hand in the ice-filled towel.

Our plight was so apparent on my way through the lobby, the bell captain started shouting directions to the hospital. By the time I got to the car, the towel was crimson, but the dress was still untouched, as if protecting it would somehow save her. Over piercing cries, her mother and I calmly assured her that it was going to be all right; something none of us believed. In the end the cut would require 25 stitches. On a three-year-old hand there isn't room for 25 stitches.

The hospital was 20 minutes away: I made it in ten, breaking every law I encountered. Finally, faced with a red light at a busy intersection, I was forced to stop, which gave me a chance to see the towel had soaked through and the valiant dress had finally succumbed. The cries had been reduced to moans and a fragile whimper. Unable to move for the moment, I decided to take a look at how bad her hand really was.

What I would do with the information, I had no idea, but somehow I had to see. With teeth clenched and breath held I reached for the towel and as I gently started to unwrap it, she stopped crying, looked up and said, "Don't look at it, Daddy…it will hurt your eyes."

What a choice of words and feelings. Of all the

possibilities of the moment, this three-year-old came out with something from a place that could only be her core, her essence, her soul: "Don't look at it, Daddy…it will hurt your eyes." So loving and unselfish.

At that moment Dana Persky won my heart, my devotion, and my support forever.

***

The twins arrived in 1968, an exotic ingredient added to a pot on a slow simmer of conflict. Their novelty was enough to take the pressure off the marriage for a while, and these weren't just twins: They were Jamie and Liza—"The Girls," as they've been known from day one. They share all the expected similarities of twins, but their personal essences, though identically pure and gentle, had very different shadings.

In 1972, when divorce was becoming an American epidemic, we were the first on our block to catch it. There was no Oprah, or Dr. Phil, to lay out the behavior, and future writers of "self-help" books hadn't yet learned to help themselves. So, we in the first wave had to make up the behavior as we went along.

Most of us weren't any better at divorce than at marriage, but, again, no blame, everybody did the best they could. We decided on "joint custody" before the term had been officially coined. If I'd have copyrighted it, at just a penny per use the royalty would have paid the alimony and child support to come.

In talking about the twins, Jamie comes first because Jamie came first, preceding Liza by five minutes: Just enough time alone to be concerned about her missing partner.

That concern for Liza's well being—make that *everyone's* well being—let's make that *every living thing's* well being—has been a constant. Consequently, she is the most gentle, or sensitive, or…I'm trying to avoid *fragile* because that word implies weakness and she's anything but. *Vulnerable* is close, but suggests too readily bruised, and that isn't her either. It's probably a bit of each that causes her to deal with things from the heart, to a point where you fear for its being broken. Although I loved her for that softness, I anguished over the hurt it would foster.

She was seven when I saw I could stop worrying and just enjoy who she was. Though gentle, sensitive and vulnerable, she was also fearless and strong: She might get hurt but she wouldn't run, she wouldn't break, and she'd never quit.

Strangely, my moment of discovery with Jamie also involved a rush to the hospital for stitches. Then, again, maybe it's not so strange. For children, that first hurt, that first open wound reveals not only the fragile nature of the flesh, but somehow a first frightening awareness of their vulnerability. What better moment for them to feel—and for us to see—something profound.

I was rehearsing a television special with Sonny & Cher when I got the call that Jamie had been attacked by a large dog and was in an ambulance headed for UCLA Medical Center. "Large dog" and "ambulance" were the only words I remembered from the call as I made the half-hour trip in fifteen minutes, arriving just as Jamie was being wheeled into the trauma center.

What I saw was not good: Her arm was opened from the elbow halfway to the wrist. She was still in some kind of shock, but on seeing me she just let go and started to cry. I held her throughout the surgery. Because the area had been anesthetized, her tears were not from pain, but the cumulative anxiety of what had happened and the activity of the trauma team orbiting around her.

I tried to calm her, to divert her attention, but I also really wanted to find out what had happened. She gave me an opening when, in almost a replay of her sister Dana nine years before, she pushed aside concern for herself to ask, "Are the dogs all right?"

I assured her they were fine, even though I didn't have

any idea of how or where they were. Then I asked if she wanted to tell me about what had happened.

She had been waiting to be picked up after school when a really skinny old dog came over to her. She hadn't called him or anything. I gently reminded her of how one has to be careful of strange dogs. Oh, she knew that, but this one was really nice and he looked sad. There was a piece of sandwich left in her lunch box and when she offered it to him, another big dog came up and started growling at her. The nice dog growled back to protect her. And then the big dog went after the nice dog, so she tried to stop him and he bit her.

Though comforting her, I couldn't let the moment pass without making the point that sometimes you just have to stay out of the way and not get in the middle, even with dogs you know, but especially with dogs you don't know. Did she understand that? She did. I made her promise she wouldn't do anything like that again. She did promise. Then she asked a question that I could answer with logic, but not without killing the light inside that had provoked it: "But what if I could help?"

She had already seen the consequences of getting involved, already felt the pain, and still there it was: "But what if I could help?" In that moment, I knew there were more stitches and hurts to come, but I also knew she could handle them.

And now for Liza, who, better late than never, arrived five minutes after Jamie and was well worth the wait.

There may be gynecological explanations for the delay but, knowing Liza, she was just thinking it over, already wise enough to know it was going to be tough out there, no longer just the two of them sharing and understanding one another. Maybe Jamie (though she didn't know that was her name at the time) would look things over, reach the same conclusion and come back. But after five minutes, she grew concerned that her partner might be in trouble, so out she came, and we are all better off for it.

If Dana was the poet and Jamie the healer, Liza was our Solomon, always taking the extra five minutes to see both sides, and all too often finding herself in the middle. She always possessed a wisdom beyond her years, and a feeling of responsibility for everyone else. You had to love her for it, but, as a father, you had to be concerned. I thought she was a pushover—though hardly a martyr—but she was far more ready to stand up for others than for herself.

At eight she proved me wrong.

"Joint custody" means two sets of everything: toys, clothes, even pets. At my house, The Girls had hamsters, Fresca and Happy, named for reasons or traits I don't recall. Dana had a rabbit whose twitching lips resulted in the name Bogart. Sibling rivalry is only intensified when twins are part of the equation, and heightened when the divorce follows soon after their arrival. Dana had all that and more to deal with and tried in every way to keep the twins in their place.

Bogart became a cause célèbre and The Girls were not allowed near him without Dana's permission. Being only five and not understanding the dynamic involved, The Girls caused constant consternation by sneaking Bogart into their room at every opportunity. The turmoil I endured over that rabbit surpassed anything Elmer Fudd ever experienced with Bugs Bunny. Ironically, it was thanks to Bogart that I got to have my "falling in love" with Liza experience.

I'd come from chaos at the office to disaster at home. Bogart was missing, allegations were flying, denials abounding, and tears overflowing. From the level of emotion, clearly Bogart was a metaphor. The fragile fabric of our co-existence was unraveling and I didn't want to deal with the fallout. So wisely, I started accusing and ranting along with the rest of the kids.

Finally, through her sobs, Liza admitted that she had let Bogart out of his cage so he could get some exercise. Rather than reward her for the honesty, I pounced with yet another rerun of my speech on sharing, caring, and each doing our part to make things okay. Liza was inconsolable. Here she was, the one who had done the most to make it work, feeling she was causing the downfall of our entire family structure.

The low point of my behavior—and I am ashamed to admit it, even more ashamed to have done it—was in winding up my diatribe by asking Liza how she could have been so stupid. Before I could retract the words, she was on me: the tears stopped, and, in a voice just this side of Linda Blair in *The Exorcist*, she commanded, "Don't you call me '*stupid*'! I did a wrong thing, but I am *not* stupid, and don't you ever call me 'stupid' again!"

I was stunned and embarrassed, yet secretly pleased. My stupidity had awakened a side of Liza I had never dreamed was there; compassionate to be sure, but she was hardly a pushover. I apologized profusely, as I do again, for underestimating just who she was at her core. I didn't know until that moment that an eight-year-old could also demand your respect, but she got mine that day and has never lost it. Nor has she ever lost the love that was there from day one.

Over the years I have watched my daughters grow into very special young women and every time I see them, there is the aura of those moments when I really saw them for the first time.

THE WOMEN

Daughters, mother, sister, wives, granddaughters, goddaughters, actresses—as I said, women are a core issue in my life, so it's no accident that most of my best work has been about them: Mary Tyler Moore on *The Dick Van Dyke Show* in the early 60s; Marlo Thomas in *That Girl* from '65 to '70; *Kate & Allie*, with Jane Curtin and Susan St. James, in the 80s.

In television's beginnings in the 50s, the role of women was limited to adorable daughters (Gale Storm in *My Little Margie),* elegant hostesses (Loretta Young in her eponymous show), and the dutiful, understanding, second-class citizen-wife (Marjorie Lord in *Make Room for Daddy*, Donna Reed in *The Donna Reed Show,* Jane Wyatt in *Father Knows Best,* and Barbara Billingsley in *Leave It To Beaver)*; all Moms waiting in full make-up, with proper dress and apron preparing dinner along with the problem of the day for "Him" to get home and make everything right with "His" wisdom.

There was only one rebel in the group and, hard to imagine, it was Lucy. She wanted equality, recognition, and everything Ricky had, and although she used feminine wiles during her madcap antics, she was, in her own way, television's first feminist and, behind the camera, Desi's full partner in Desilu Studios.

The Dick Van Dyke Show was a step forward with the

wife as a peer: Although Laura was afraid of upsetting Rob, he was equally afraid of upsetting *her*, and he was hardly an authority figure in the relationship. It was probably a reflection of the great respect Carl Reiner had for his wife, Estelle, more than a shift in the social dynamic, but the public loved the show and the role of women on television started to change.

The first real breakthrough was getting ABC to buy *That Girl* in 1965—a single girl living on her own in New York City, wanting a career and not trying to get married???

Impossible!!

I would note that in 1965 the only woman in the room was Marlo: none of the three networks had a female executive in programming at that time. But Marlo developed an ally in one of the great network executives of that, or any time, Edgar Scherick.

THE VELVET
STEAMROLLER

I dubbed Marlo Thomas "The Velvet Steamroller" with the greatest of affection. She could roll over you but not hurt you in the process, and, as much as I can take credit for the creation of *That Girl*, it was her determination and commitment that made the show a reality.

I will, however, take full credit for the title and the opening shot that became the show's signature. The original title was "*Miss Independence*," which her father, Danny, called her as she stood up to him—probably with the first words to come out of her mouth. Danny Thomas was a formidable guy both on stage and off, but Marlo never backed down in their constant head-on collisions as she, his female counterpart, asserted her own views and made her own decisions. Their love for one another was fierce, as was their love of battle. Marlo, like *That Girl*, had moved out of the family home—something Danny couldn't understand given that she wasn't getting married or becoming a nun. The first night on her own, she called in panic when she discovered her apartment was overrun with ants. Danny proclaimed to the rest of the family: "Miss Independence has ants."

Somehow, though, it never felt right as the title. It was cute, but not really the character we had created. Ann Marie was not so much declaring her independence as asserting her right as a person to create her own path in her own way. She was like my sister, Bunny, who was the image I had in mind as I wrote. Just like Marlo, she was always her own person, with her own values who is, as I introduced her at a testimonial dinner: "My sister Bunny, a combination of Golda Meir, Auntie Mame and Peter Pan." She perplexed my conservative parents to the point that they referred to her in the third person: "You can't believe what that girl is doing now!" "That girl is driving me crazy!"

"That girl" also became the solution to a problem we had in writing the pilot. We had to quickly establish the multiple sides of Ann Marie: the daughter, the aspiring actress, and the girl trying to pay the rent. We did it in three quick scenes: with her parents, after a phone call telling them she was up for a big part, looking at a very serious Ann Marie in cap and gown, and proudly saying, "There is no stopping that girl"; then a publicity shot of an animated and beautiful Ann Marie as her agent says, "The perfect one for the part is that girl"; to a scene in a restaurant where an annoyed patron asks a passing busboy, "Who is my waitress?" and the busboy points to a frazzled-looking Ann Marie, her cap askew and her tray about to fall, and says, "That girl." The camera zoomed into a close-up of the face that would become the inspiration for millions of American girls, and change the landscape for women on television and in our society.

The biggest fight we had with the network was the executives' insistence that Ann Marie and her boyfriend, Don, get married on the last episode. Marlo refused and fought passionately, feeling that saying at the end, "It's all about getting married," was not what the series was about. Supported by countless letters of admiration, and the addition of a couple of young women to the program department, once again, the Velvet Steamroller flattened the opposition. She isn't easy but she is smart, fair, loyal and a great friend. In 2006 when I was awarded a Lifetime Achievement Award from the Writer's Guild, not only was she there, but she was also the hit of the evening when she presented the award and sang a song she had written for me. I treasure Marlo Thomas, and in a crisis, she is like having my own Seal Team 6.

That Girl, both the person and the show, is a high point in my life and career. In addition, it made me a hero to women in their 40's 50's and 60's, women whose lives were changed by the show's message. Also, for some reason, the show was important to gay men—I think it was the clothes.

MARY AND ME

In 1970, Mary Tyler Moore came through the door Marlo had opened, arriving as a single woman (though she still couldn't be divorced) with no parents nearby, and she was out in the dating world that, with each season, grew bolder as the career world grew more inclusive. At that point the networks realized that women were a big part of their audience and started hiring some women executives. It was difficult to be the first into the testosterone-studded meetings so the women had to walk a fine line: tough and strong meant they were labeled "ballsy dykes" or "bitches"; feminine or sexy, "manipulative"; empathetic and understanding meant "weak". I remember meetings with some of the early female executives and it wasn't easy on them or me; they hadn't yet found a way to just be themselves. The one thing I could count on: the more Laura Ashley and white wicker in the office, the tougher the female executive would be. That was the atmosphere in which *The Mary Tyler Moore Show* came to be. Though I wasn't involved in doing the show, according to Mary, I helped make it possible.

After the *Van Dyke Show* ended in 1965, all of us involved were golden. We had plenty of opportunities—offers to do whatever we wanted. Mary and Dick had movie contracts: him with Disney; her at Universal where she was to be the next Doris Day. It was everything any actress could hope for...well, any actress except Mary. Her dream had always been to star in a Broadway musical, and she got her chance when she was offered the part of Holly Golightly in the stage version of *Breakfast at Tiffany's*.

The show turned out to be one of the biggest flops in Broadway history, and closed before it even opened. It was produced at a time when Broadway looked down on television, so all the blame was heaped on Mary. (I saw it in Boston, and she was fantastic.) It hurt her both personally and professionally. She needed a comeback and fortunately Sam and I were in a position to help. We were doing a series of television specials for Dick Van Dyke and I suggested that because it was the fifth anniversary of the last show, it was time for a reunion. Dick enthusiastically agreed, and *Dick Van Dyke and the Other Woman* aired in April of 1969. CBS fell in love with her all over again—along with America.

My love affair with Mary had started long before: with her legs on an Old Gold commercial in 1956, then her legs—with a voice added—on the *Richard Diamond: Private Detective* television series. When the rest of her emerged on *Van Dyke*, I was joined by just about every other man in America.

Getting to know and write for her was an added bonus in what I've already mentioned was the most important thing that ever happened for me: working on *The Dick Van Dyke Show*. Right from the start, we had a special relationship and, after both her show and her marriage had ended—and she was probably the most loved woman in America, next to the Statue of Liberty—I was one of the few people she knew in New York, so we spent a lot of time together. I remember walking down the street with her one day in SoHo, and when we stopped at a traffic light, I happened to look back and it was like that old E.F. Hutton commercial where everyone was transfixed, staring at her...and yet here she was alone for the first time in her life.

Because she was single and invited to everything, for a while I became her "date," although every major New York guy was on line waiting for her to notice. Finally she noticed Warren Beatty, and our last date was the opening of *42nd Street* on Broadway. There were hundreds of photographers at the Winter Garden, and as our limo arrived, they became one: all focused on Mary. I helped her out of the car and stepped aside as they surrounded her. When I arrived home, I had a dozen messages on my machine asking why I had stepped clear of the shots. The answer was a lesson I had learned, in 1957, while eating a pastrami sandwich.

THE PASTRAMI SANDWICH
THAT CHANGED MY LIFE

It wasn't the sandwich itself. It was good, a little fatty, but good. The truth is I've had better, but never one as meaningful. I realize it's pretentious to call a pastrami sandwich meaningful. The turkey club I almost ordered would have been just as significant because it wasn't the actual sandwich, but the circumstances surrounding the pastrami that were important.

In 1955, my job at WNEW was paying $50 a week - a fortune back then - which covered food and shelter, a car, clothes, even summer weekends in the yet-to-be-chic Hamptons. Things were great, and in six months they would be even better when a promised $10 raise to $60 meant I could get married. I dreamed of making a hundred a week and would have made a deal with the devil to earn my age every year.

It was a great time that brought with it great friends. The closest were Sam Denoff, and William B. Williams, the hottest disk jockey in the country at a time when disk jockeys really mattered. We had laugh-filled lunches every day; Chinese at Billy Gwon's, Italian at Patsy's or Rocky Lee's, delicatessen at The Stage, and, at least once a week, for real laughs, The Friars.

But on the day of the pastrami sandwich, I found myself having lunch alone, and though it was my choice, I felt left out. The rest of the guys were having lunch with Frank Sinatra.

Sam was just tagging along. I'd been asked, but had

declined, although William B. had assured me that Frank wouldn't mind. After all, Sinatra owed William B. a lot. In the early 50s, when Sinatra had been considered finished, Willy B. kept playing his records, creating a Sinatra cult and labeling him, "The Chairman of the Board." If anyone was important to Sinatra, it was Willy B. and I knew I was missing out on a good time. But a place where someone "wouldn't mind" that I was "tagging along" was a place I didn't want to be.

What's so wrong with tagging along? Lots of great things happen when you're just tagging along. But for some reason, it wasn't good enough for me. I needed Frank to say, "Hey, don't forget to bring Billy." So, I gave up a chance to have lunch with Frank Sinatra.

To do what? "Whatever I want! I'm alone for lunch. Great! I don't have to worry about what anyone else wants, just me, because I'm alone for lunch."

Suddenly, I couldn't think of a food in the world I wanted, or even *liked*.

"The hell with it. I'll skip lunch."

Obviously, there was something deeper involved and having a great lunch had become a challenge. I decided on The Stage Delicatessen. They weren't called "delis" then. The short form wouldn't have done justice to The Stage—not just the incredible food, which in later years led to countless triple bipasses, but the ambiance and, especially, the waiters.

"Gimme a pistol and call the doctor." That wasn't a threat, just Ernie shouting out my order: pastrami on rye, mustard only, and a Dr. Brown's Cel-Ray tonic. Most of the sandwiches had celebrity names: the Perry Como (tuna, tomato, and Swiss cheese); the Mickey Mantle (boiled ham, Muenster cheese, and Russian dressing); the Tony Martin (corned beef, chopped liver, onion, and chicken fat). If you wanted to know who was a star in the 50s, forget *Variety* - just check the bill of fare at The Stage.

The owner, Max Asnas, was a short, fat guy who loved his own food and adored athletes and show people. In tribute, his menu commemorated greatness in cold cuts, mustard, and for his non-Jewish clientele, mayo. He once air-lifted lox and bagels to Elizabeth Taylor in Italy while she was making *Cleopatra* and sturgeon for Richard Burton, who was making her.

Every columnist in New York mentioned The Stage every day, and for the tourists, it was right next to the Statue of Liberty as a "thing to see" in New York. The walls were covered with pictures of Max in the company of his famous patrons. Not caricatures or anything cute, but real pictures of real guys at golf tournaments, Vegas dressing rooms, World Series, prize fights, The Kentucky Derby, opening night at The Copa. Max was always there in the middle of the action, and had the pictures to prove it.

Being there alone, I had a chance to study those pictures, and at a table for one rather than our usual four, I was face-to-face with a great shot of Dean Martin, Jerry Lewis, Bing Crosby, Joe DiMaggio, Max, and some guy I didn't recognize on the first tee at Pebble Beach. Everyone was laughing and obviously having a great time—except the guy next to Max, the one I didn't recognize.

I got closer to read the caption: "The Crosby 1954. Dean Martin, Jerry Lewis, Bing Crosby, Joe DiMaggio, Max Asnas, and an unidentified stranger."

No wonder he wasn't smiling. What a sad thing to be: an unidentified stranger. There it was, that was it, why I wasn't having lunch with Frank Sinatra, why I didn't want to tag along and have Frank not mind.

Like the walls of The Stage, my father's office was filled with pictures of him with celebrities, the difference being that none of them had had any idea who my father was or even that their picture was being taken with him. He had a way of getting in the frame and looking for all the world as if he belonged. He was so good at that: the celebrities seemed to be in the picture with him. It always made me uncomfortable as he worked his way into position for my mother to get the shot. I defy you to see those pictures and not believe that he was a "friend to the stars."

He played it beautifully whenever customers came into his office, never pointing to the gallery, but waiting for them to discover the photos, always underplaying but creating the impression: "Look who I know and therefore, who I must be."

I knew that was someone I never wanted to be, in places I didn't belong, and my approach has worked out pretty well. Only in my pursuit of love and romance have I been in places and pictures where I was an unidentified stranger, especially to myself.

THE AUTOMATIC TOASTER

I wasn't planning to include any stories about my father, but when Carl Reiner read an early draft, he couldn't believe I left out his two favorites and insisted I include them. Feel free to come back to them, ignore them, or trust Carl that they are worth reading.

Carl never actually met my father, but became a fan of his while he, Sam, and I were writing "The Plots Thicken," a *Van Dyke* episode about Rob's father buying a cemetery plot with room for him and Laura. It went on to be a war with Laura's family about who was going to be buried with whom. Since Rob's father hadn't been on the show up to that point, we started to create him. I mentioned that my father had a trait we could use: he never let an opportunity go to waste when he could make a flowery toast. I dubbed him "Jerry Persky, the automatic toaster: Put a glass in his hand and he pops up." Actually, *any* kind of liquid in *any* kind of vessel could set him off. Once he was taking a tablespoon of medicine and said, "I take this in the hope none of you will ever know this kind of sickness."

He was shameless and if I doubted his sincerity, I couldn't his originality. He made his most unusual toast on his first visit to L.A. soon after we'd bought our first house and just as workmen were finishing the pool.

As the toasting gods would have it, while I was at work,

he got to be the first person to go in. I knew the event would be memorable and, though I missed it, I can picture it vividly: him standing on the edge of the pool, his arms spread like a high priest, looking heavenward and intoning, "I christen this the pool of happiness and love," followed by a less than poetic dive.

A MAN WHO NEEDS
NO INTRODUCTION

In the 50s, two American girls married into royalty: Grace Kelly to Prince Rainier of Monaco, and my sister Bunny to the lesser-known Jewish prince, Paul Grossinger of the famed Grossinger's Catskills Resort Hotel. Though less regal, Bunny got the better deal because Grossinger's was probably bigger than Monaco and the food had to have been a lot better.

The Catskills back then were the Hamptons of today and the Mecca for stars of show business and sports. A given weekend would find Mickey Mantle and Rocky Marciano sitting poolside with Eddie Fisher and Elizabeth Taylor, Milton Berle, Dean Martin and Jerry Lewis. It was a dream world for all of us, and my father's picture gallery was running out of space.

In the summer of 1955, there was a charity golf tournament at the hotel with some of the biggest pros and celebrities taking part. I was working at WNEW at the time, and William B. Williams, the hottest disk jockey in the country, was invited. Since I was going, I invited Sam to come as well.

Of course my father wouldn't miss the event and, since none of my friends had met him, I went to great lengths preparing them for his predictably unpredictable behavior. They assured me that all fathers are a little nuts and to stop worrying, which I did, until the owner of the station, an avid golfer and the "King of the WASPs," invited himself to join us. Because my father was the self-appointed "King of the Jews," my potential embarrassment was reaching Biblical proportions.

Our group arrived in time for the Friday evening welcoming cocktail party at my sister's house, filled with stars of stage and screen, but minus my father, meaning he would get to make an entrance: always a challenge. We were in the den at the far end of a long living room when my sister said, "Dad!"

I went into a catatonic state, knowing that with such a big and important a crowd he was not about to miss the opportunity for an entrance. Never one to disappoint, when he appeared at the other end of the living room and spotted me, he dropped to a defensive linemen's four-point stance, barked out, "Hut Hut *Hut,"* and came barreling the full length of the room—about 50 feet— hitting me at the knees and taking me down in a perfect tackle.

When we finished rolling, I calmly looked up at the shocked faces of my friends and said, "Guys, I'd like you to meet my father."

KATE & ALLIE

By 1982, shows about women and female executives were abundant, but *Kate & Allie,* a show about two divorced women and their children living together was a breakthrough. Just as *That Girl* had been a turning point in the way young women began to think about their options, so *Kate & Allie* provided insight for the ever-increasing number of divorced women coping with new financial and social realities.

As a single parent myself, raising my oldest daughter on my own from the time she was 12, I had firsthand knowledge of the difficulty of trying to be both mother and father. I will never forget the looks I got as the only man in the waiting room at Dana's first gynecological appointment. Jane Curtin and Susan St. James, as Kate & Allie respectively, became role models for countless women sharing the highs and lows of this social development, letting them smile and even laugh at the absurdity of it all.

A career in television comedy provides a lot of good things but very seldom a feeling of satisfaction that what you are doing really matters. But I got to experience that feeling on *That Girl,* seeing the thousands of letters from teenagers describing how the show had changed their lives and then again on *Kate & Allie* with letters from divorced women who were rebuilding theirs. Of them all I kept just one.

It was during the second season, from Beverly in

Minnesota, who wrote: "I am recently divorced, have no skills or training, two kids and am scared to death. Thank you for letting me know I'm not crazy and I'm not alone."

In a less serious vein, a psychiatrist friend told me about one of his patients whose ex-husband had recently been remarried to a younger, very successful woman, and with Thanksgiving approaching, she was anxiety-ridden about how to handle the holiday. Should the kids go to their father's? Should she have her own dinner? Should they have two dinners?

He expected more of the same at her next appointment, but she never mentioned it. Finally he asked, "And what's happening with Thanksgiving?"

She matter-of-factly told him: "I'm going to do what Kate & Allie did. I'm cooking, they're coming, and whatever happens, happens."

The world had come a long way in 20 years.

BOOKENDS

I look at *That Girl* and *Kate & Allie* as bookends in the changing role of women on television, with Mary Tyler Moore in the middle.

There were the tentative first steps by Marlo, to the strides by Mary, and the no-holds-barred sprint of Susan & Jane. I think the clearest way to show this evolution is with the episode of the clogged sink.

Each series had one and the way the story went in each case clearly illustrates my point: On *That Girl*, Ann Marie called her father; Mary called a plumber; Kate & Allie tried to fix it themselves, flooded the apartment, then called a plumber and Kate had an affair with him for eight shows, breaking it off when he wanted to get married. From there, Murphy Brown was an unwed mother, and on *Friends*, everybody had sex with everybody.

During *The Dick Van Dyke Show* the censors wouldn't let us use the word "pregnant." No matter how hard Carl fought and reasoned, they refused, saying some people still told their children babies were delivered by the stork or found behind cabbages, and we didn't have the right to go into those people's homes and have their children ask: "What is pregnant?" Carl responded that those people didn't deserve to have children or homes.

Of course today those former children are being asked by *their* children: "What is a four-hour erection?" And what does it mean: "when the moment is right"? I wonder if any of those parents has the answer to my question: "What are those two people doing in that bathtub?"

LIFE DOESN'T
IMITATE ART

In the years I did those shows, I won five Emmys and was considered "The Guy" on the subject of women, while in real life I had ended one marriage of 14 years, another marriage of five, and had been involved in several disastrous relationships. I was doing better with women on paper than in real life. For the record, I blame no one but myself for any of the failed relationships I have shared or caused. As I recount them, the names are changed to protect the innocent, the guilty, and those who were just passing through. In fairness, I acknowledge these stories are all from my point of view, clouded by time, but softened with the awareness that nobody ever set out to hurt anybody, and the pain caused was mostly in self-defense.

Also from this vantage point, I am totally forgiving of anything done unto me and hope that the doers will be equally forgiving of that which was done unto them.

LOVE AND MARRIAGE #1:
"LOVE"

Though I had the usual high school and college romances, including a fraternity pinning complete with a moonlit serenade in a howling blizzard, I don't think any of the events before my first marriage really count, nor do they bear retelling. Well, maybe the pinning and serenade because 60 years later I am still embarrassed that they actually happened, but pinning and serenading was reflective of the period that shaped dating and marriage in the 50s.

It was like a scene from a bad college movie starring Van Johnson as me and June Allison as her. The high, or low, point was my solo of the "Fraternity Sweetheart Song" as 40 drunken "brothers" and her sobbing "sisters" hummed softly in the background. In the end, the relationship was as stormy as the night, and my pin, which was attached to hers by a gold chain, went back and forth so often I eventually kept pliers in the glove compartment of my car because undoing the clasp by hand was taking a heavy toll on my fingernails.

I offer this scenario not with pride but in the interest of full disclosure as to how good I was with women going back to my first kiss with Esther Kastoriniss during a game of "mailman" at her eighth birthday party and then worrying that she had become pregnant. I didn't know what that meant but Jerry Marks told me if she was, my life would be ruined forever. I doubt I was much better informed, or prepared, 20 years later when I embarked on my first marriage.

LOVE AND MARRIAGE #2:
"THE CHOCOLATE WEDDING CAKE"

In 1956, the year of my first wedding, no bride could have a chocolate wedding cake. They weren't illegal, but they broke the architectural laws of pastry. Apparently, to support the weight of the upper tiers and the little portico holding the bride and groom on top, there had to be a more substantial base than chocolate would allow. Your frosting, rosettes, garlands, bells, hearts and cupids could be any color you chose, but a stress-per-layer physics formula governed the actual cake and called for a cement-like mix of pound cake laced with nuts and dried fruit.

If I know too much about chocolate wedding cakes it's because, despite the protestations of the caterers and several bakeries, Linda, my soon-to-be bride, was determined to have one and did an exhaustive, unrelenting and, in retrospect, obsessive research project to prove existing wedding cake standards unacceptable. I should have taken that as an omen, and as our marriage turned out, we should have considered a lot more than the cake. But in the 50s things didn't work that way, which is probably why, of the 10 weddings I attended back then, only three made it through the 70s. Of course, there wasn't much pre-marital sex, and if there was to be *any*, the first step was down the aisle.

When Linda grudgingly accepted that you couldn't have a three-tiered cake with a bride and groom on top without using the standard pound cake, fruit, and nut substructure, I set out on my own quest for the Chocolate Grail. I suspected then—and know now—it was less about pleasing her than about proving how wonderful *I* was.

My plan was to get a regular chocolate cake, put a bride and groom on top, and have it waiting in our room at the Forest Hills Inn where we were to spend our wedding night before leaving for our honeymoon in Bermuda. (In the 50s you weren't legally married without going to Bermuda.)

Two weeks before the wedding, I put the plan in motion, starting at the Metropolitan Bakery in Forest Hills. It was crowded, as usual, so I took a number and checked out cakes in the display case. There was one decorated for "Malcolm on his 8th Birthday" with a plastic Mickey Mantle on top. That cake would be perfect if I substituted a bride and groom for Mickey.

I heard my number—"63!"—called out in a heavy German accent, and followed the voice to Sophie, an elderly saleslady, diminutive enough to be atop a cake herself. I told her I wanted a chocolate wedding cake and she said I couldn't have one and started on why.

I assured her I knew all the reasons and just wanted a cake like Malcolm's with a bride and groom on top to surprise my new wife who had her heart set on a chocolate wedding cake.

Sophie, a fellow romantic, fell instantly in love, gave me a brownie and took me to Harriet. "Tell her what you want, darling."

When I said a chocolate wedding cake, Harriet said I couldn't have one and started on why until Sophie took over: "He knows, he knows, tell her the rest."

When I did, Harriet also fell in love, gave me a black and white cookie, and they took me to Edna, another cookie, then Selma, a Danish. By the time I got to Gus, the head baker, I was Darling Billy who is marrying a wonderful Linda, a Phi Beta Kappa no less, and he wants a chocolate wedding cake, which, of course, he told me I couldn't have. After Sophie and the girls filled him in, Gus took over.

There would be not just a "Malcolm cake" with a bride and groom on top, but a hand-crafted, heart-shaped Gus original, and if I brought in our pictures, Sophie would personally paste our faces on the bride and groom. If this cake caused as much good feeling with the bride as it did with the staff of the Metropolitan Bakery, our future marital happiness was assured.

With the cake resolved, my next step was to alert the staff of the Forest Hills Inn. I started with Kevin, the assistant manager, explaining that the Metropolitan Bakery would deliver a wedding cake on Saturday , and I wanted it placed on the bed in our room. He looked at me as if I was planning something illegal, so I explained about the chocolate wedding cake, we went through the you-can't-have-one ritual, and in the end he just loved the whole thing and said he would include a bottle of champagne and flowers from the hotel. I gave him five dollars to seal the deal and got the names of staff that would be involved. Another five to Ronnie the bellboy, Chris the elevator man, and Francine, the head of housekeeping, and I had all fronts covered. I returned to the Metropolitan Bakery, where they greeted me like a long-lost son, and I gave Sophie all the contacts at the hotel. I offered her a five; she refused and gave me a cupcake.

For a wedding I had approached with trepidation, suddenly I couldn't wait—not for the wedding, but for the adoration that would consume my new wife when she saw her cake. (I didn't go with our faces on the bride and groom, feeling that was too gimmicky).

April 15th dawned bright and sunny, as did I in anticipation. The wedding was typical: a ceremony that ran too long, followed by the cocktail hour featuring a chopped liver mold, pigs in blankets, and a Cupid ice sculpture, then a roast beef or chicken dinner, depending on the affluence of the bride's parents, toasts, the Hora, kids sliding across the floor and dancing while standing on the grandfather's shoes, and finally the cutting of the cake. As we jointly made our ceremonial cut revealing the standard pound cake base, Linda whispered her disappointment that it wasn't chocolate, and I couldn't have been more excited about my thoughtfulness.

By midnight I was obsessed with getting to the hotel, an urgency which judging from the leers and sly comments, everyone thought was about sex. Why would they think it was about cake? I drove at breakneck speed, which she probably thought was about sex. On checking in, the clerk gave us a sly wink, and she blushed, thinking it was about sex. I winked back knowing it was about cake.

As we approached our room, I couldn't decide whether to open the door to let her go in first and see it or if I should go in first and just step aside dramatically to reveal the cake. I decided on opening the door and carrying her across the threshold so she would already have her arms around my neck when she saw it, making it easier for her to embrace me with joy, love, and gratitude.

As I picked her up, we both laughingly entered the room, I turned toward the bed and there it…*wasn't*. The bed was empty.

In a spontaneous response, I uttered a guttural, "Shit!!!" dropped her on the bed and stormed out, leaving her sitting alone in the room wondering what she had gotten herself into. (It wouldn't be the last time she would wonder about that over the next 14 years.)

Since we were on the second floor, I charged down the stairs to confront the desk clerk who was visibly shaken by the fury of my approach. I growled: "Where is my cake?" and he backed up further. In an incoherent rant, I went through the history of my plan and how the hotel had failed me.

Although he had no idea what I was raving about, he immediately defended the hotel. I countered that it couldn't have been Sophie and the gang at the bakery because the chocolate wedding cake had become more important to them than to me. It was *his* people: Chris the elevator man, Ronnie the bellboy, Francine from housekeeping, and *especially* Kevin, the assistant manager who had all loved the whole idea. Somehow he managed to piece together that it had something to do with a cake.

"Not just a cake! A *chocolate* wedding cake!"

He started to say there was no such thing, but my look warned him off.

The level of our exchange managed to attract Norman, the night janitor who looked older than the hotel. With the clerk explaining and me fuming, Norman not only understood, but also had the answer.

"You're the guy with the cake? Where were you?"

"Where was I? I'm right here! Where's my cake?"

"It's down in the storeroom."

"Why wasn't it on the bed where it was supposed to be?"

"Why weren't *you* here like *you* were supposed to be?"

"I'm *here!* This is *I!*"

Then, Norman stopped me cold. "But where were you last Saturday when they delivered the cake? We were all set! Kevin, Ronnie, Chris, Francine—and you never showed up!"

As we made our way to the storeroom, I realized what had happened. Not wanting to wait until the last minute, I had gone to the bakery a week ago. We had all gotten so caught up in the plan that I never got around to telling them the date of the wedding, and since I had gone in on a Thursday, they just assumed it was for that Saturday. It was not the first time, nor the last, that my excitement over the big picture caused me to lose sight of the more mundane things like where and when.

As we entered the poorly-lit room, there were all manner of suitcases, cartons, packages, trunks, and racks of clothes, but nothing looked so out of place and lost as the grease-stained Metropolitan Bakery box sitting sadly off by itself.

I gave Norman a five, and before heading back to the room, stopped to look at my ill-fated surprise. The cake and frosting were stale and had hardened, but not before the bride and groom had sunk up to their noses. To my surprise, Linda wasn't in tears but opening a bottle of champagne the desk clerk had brought up along with a rough explanation of what had happened. I handed her the box with a dejected, "Here's your damn chocolate wedding cake."

She appreciated the thought, and we actually ate a piece. As I looked at the sunken bride and groom peering out over the frosting, I was glad our faces weren't attached, as that would have made the entire cake saga tragic rather than just stupid.

LOVE AND MARRIAGE #3:
"MARRIAGE IN THE 50's"

I was 22. She was 21. And although it lasted 14 years, it started going wrong right after the "I do's" because we didn't. We didn't know we didn't, and actually thought we did, and then tried to, but couldn't, because we didn't understand what was actually involved.

Like many couples, we were part of a 50's mentality: If you weren't married by 23 and parents by 25, you could be called before Joe McCarthy for being un-American. So "I," with no idea of who I was, joined "her," who had no idea who *she* was, and set out to find happiness as "us," whoever *we* were. It was like trying to make $1 + 1 = 1$: mathematically impossible and emotionally difficult.

We both grew and added new dimensions and interests, all of which threatened the "oneness." I tried to get her to add my things, while she was doing the same, which meant we were attempting to make $5 + 5 = 1$, mathematically and emotionally impossible, but we worked at it for 14 years.

Just in passing, it has been my experience through diligently "working at" a number of relationships, that there is an important difference between "working at" and struggling: you work to create something, and struggle to survive it.

During our struggle, we managed to create three wonderful daughters who are worth whatever else came of our union. Without any details that might embarrass them.

Without placing blame: there was very little romance in the relationship, and I remember the moment I knew there had to be something better.

We were at a golf outing in Pebble Beach, as I've already mentioned, one of the most beautiful sites in America. After buying a case of wine at a local vineyard, the owner gave us a gift bottle and two glasses to drink on the beach as we watched the sunset. I found a spot where the waves were huge and perfectly formed as they crested and broke, the turquoise water so clear you could see the sunset through it. Picasso would have been impressed.

We leaned against a perfectly-sculpted piece of driftwood and sipped the wine with gulls providing the background music, and I remember thinking, *if someone told me about this, it would sound terrific.*

MR. ROMANCE

Being a romantic has gotten me into trouble financially, emotionally, and in this case, physically. I was one breath away from being stoned, flayed, or at the bare minimum, hated to death by a group of middle-aged, over-privileged men mutually seeking a higher plane at a therapy group in Beverly Hills during the winter of 1969. The date, season, and place are important for an understanding of the angst, which had brought us together.

Beverly Hills was really enough all by itself: a constant mirror reflecting that no matter how good you looked or what you had, someone always looked better and had more. It is the only place on earth where you could leave a five million dollar house in a $100,000 car and, after six blocks, feel like a complete failure: especially if you were in "The Business," as all but one of our group was. The freeways were crowded with people in the morning going to do something, and at night, coming home from doing it. Well, whatever it was, we believed they only did what they did because they couldn't be in "The Business." That was just one of the distortions of reality that brought us to that Beverly Hills room every Wednesday at 3:00 p.m.

Winter is significant because most of us were transplanted New Yorkers and, therefore, had a floating anxiety due to the lack of seasonal changes for which Los Angeles is loved by some and hated by others. It gave no external help to place you, and therefore, your interests, clothing, and pursuits in context. In Los Angeles, you can do anything you want any time of the year, which is maddening. That fact was most evident in winter because it's a "non-season" season, neither cold enough, hot enough, wet enough, nor dry enough to tell your emotional clock where you were in the year, and as a result, where you were in your life. If you woke from a six-month coma on an L.A. winter's day, you would have no climactic sign to help orient yourself.

January, February, and March are just the names of months and not chapter headings for a time when people in more temperate climates were, like the flowers, migrant birds, and fruits of the vine, in a period of repose, reflection, and replenishment. There was no snow, cold, or short days of early darkness to have you longing for the spring and the new beginning for everything in nature. You were in constant limbo. Of course "The Business" had its seasons: development, pilot, selling, and waiting, but those "seasons" only added to the uncertainty.

1969 brought its own anxiety to the mix. Morals, perceptions, and lifestyles were changing as fast as the rush from the "sex, drugs and rock & roll" was fueling them. It was a time of "anything goes," and everyone went right along with the anything. Gone were restraint, tradition, dignity, and the value system that had held us all together. "If a marriage falls in the forest and nobody cares, is anyone hurt?" The children, of course, but they were asked to understand. They didn't, and neither did we, but who cared? Marriages were out, and the search for a relationship was in.

My divorce was still a year away, but all the ingredients were simmering, and it was only a matter of time until they boiled over. I don't know if I went to the group as a means of working to avoid it or seeking a vote of confidence to support it. Again, the 60s were a time when questions no one had ever asked were being answered, and the right to personal happiness and pleasure could have easily passed as the 29th Amendment.

Sex was everywhere and if it wasn't in your marital bed, you had a "get out of jail free card" to go seek it. The entire group was stuck with a moral code and tradition, however, that spelled G-U-I-L-T. We had come together to roll "emotional doubles" and get the card, or to make things work where we were: F-E-A-R-OF-C-H-A-N-G-E.

I was in a marriage that, after 14 years, was bringing neither of us much happiness: my wife was looking for a sense of herself and a level of expression that was still three years away with the advent of Women's Liberation. (She has always been ahead of her time.)

My wants were more elusive. I was searching for wonder and a woman who would love, respect, cherish, adore, and accept me for who I was and who I wasn't.

If you are looking for any of the above, let me save you a lot of time and trouble: you are supposed to get them from *yourself.* Knowing that earlier would have made life a lot simpler and this book a lot shorter.

Everyone in the room those Wednesday afternoons was as much a "type" as a person, starting with Dr. Shlecter, our therapist, who had actually known Freud. It would have been more helpful if he had read, studied, or understood Freud, but since this was L.A., knowing Freud was a better credit. The rest of us were "Children of the Depression"—the country's economic, and our parents' emotional. The country recovered in the early 40s, but my father's lingered on.

We were all respected members of the show business community with six Emmys and four Academy Awards among us, earning more money than we had ever dreamed possible, and it just wasn't enough. I am more embarrassed to write that sentence today than I was to feel it then.

Tom, the real estate tycoon, presented a refreshing difference because he was younger than the rest of us and had actually been born in California. (I knew there must have been people who were, but had never seen one up close; there is superstition that if you meet two in one day, you make a wish, and if you then see three women in a row with un-augmented breasts, the wish will come true.) I found Tom particularly interesting because he had found wonder, love and respect, was appreciated, cherished, adored—everything I wanted—and yet was *still* miserable. Apparently everything had come too easily and when he didn't cherish and adore back, she left. To hear him talk— or actually whimper and sob—she was also the most beautiful, sexual, desirable woman in the world. He had had it all. In fact, to see the faces of the other guys when he spoke of her, he had had enough to go around. Even Dr. Shlecter was moved at one point to offer the profound insight that Tom was an asshole. Maybe Dr. Schlecter *had* read Freud!

As the rest of "the boys" rambled from point to point, complaint to complaint, searching for a theme to their misery, Tom and I had found ours and became the focus of the sessions. We pushed each other to the edge: me with sighs for the romance I sought and him with sobs for the one he'd lost. No matter how high I reached to describe the feeling of longing, he was there to smash right back at me with a deep guttural gasp of, "I know, I know." It was like Connors and McEnroe at the finals of Wimbledon, chasing each other all over the court, making one impossible shot after another only to have each shot returned with something even better.

Given that much of what I described in my quest for romance was lyric if not poetic, I was asked to be more specific by Fred, the lawyer in the group. Myron, the accountant, and Bernie, the agent, also weren't really clear. Todd, the network executive, and Hank, the studio VP, as you might expect, wouldn't declare themselves. As a writer/producer/director, I took the challenge.

"I want to be with someone warm and lovable, beautiful, I hope, but also bright and funny."

Todd said if I found her, his network would give her a series in a choice time slot.

Bernie said he had a new client who was looking for a series and would call him when he got back to the office.

Fred offered to handle the legal, and Myron, the tax implications.

Dr. Shlecter wanted a royalty for bringing us all together.

That settled, I continued.

"Just being together is all she wants...sitting, doing nothing special, just...being together, being enough...some great music playing, a fire going, not even talking and then...just kind of looking up and still, without a word, moving, no, floating... to a spot in front of the fire." They were riveted. "She's beyond beautiful...the reflections of the flames dance across her hair... and in her eyes...all soft and warm...I could see me." At that point, Tom started to cry and begged me to stop torturing him. I had taken my best shot and he came to the net and put me away.

Whoever Tom's "She" was, even my fantasies couldn't compete. It became clear "She" was an actress, much sought after and successful. Yet, with all the fuss "the business" made over her, all she had wanted was Tom, and he'd blown it. How do you live with that? "She" probably would have left eventually, lost to the seduction of the Hollywood scene, but that's easier: Then you're just a poor soul and not a schmuck.

Tom was the most tortured human being I had ever seen and became the major concern of our meetings. Even with my competitive nature, I had to back off, and though my needs were vital for me, it was clear they weren't for the rest of the group. It was all about Tom and things got more philosophical and clinical as Dr. Shlecter went Jungian on us with archetypes and a lot of other stuff that had nothing to do with the fact that I was unhappy.

I became less hopeful that the group was my answer and started to lose interest, actually skipping a session and deciding not to go back at all. In truth, no one but Tom understood what I was looking for or thought it was really important. I began to question it myself: wonder, romance, adoring and being adored— *Get over it!*

Then, one night, I saw it.

I actually saw it happen, everything I was trying to convey, everything I wanted to experience. It wasn't a fantasy, it was *real:* two people creating magic with, and for, one another.

I had to go back to the group and "share it." Romance and wonder were out there for all of us to find, and for Tom to find again.

I arrived early for the next session, taking a chair and commanding the attention of the circle. I told Dr. Shlecter I had something really important to tell the group. He, in turn, had something important to tell me. Since I hadn't called to cancel the last session, I had to pay for it. Clearly he had read Freud.

I refused since it was a group. *I* had read *Portnoy's Complaint.* The others filtered in, and, as was the procedure in group therapy, we just kind of nodded our greetings, saving any conversation for the session itself.

The meeting started slowly and I was about to liven it up when, out of nowhere, Hank announced he was gay. Just like that! No preamble, just blurted it out.

There was a moment of shocked silence, and then an outpouring of support that was beautiful to behold even if the hugs were a little guarded.

Hank had always known something wasn't right, he said, but today it had all become clear. What a breakthrough! Unquestionably the biggest thing to happen in the group. The rest of Hank's life might be uncertain, but for that group, that day, he was the man of the hour…the *whole* hour.

I had a great moment of my own to share and Hank was crowding me out. I began to resent him: a whole life of being gay and he had to pick *today* to realize it.

With about ten minutes left and everyone emotionally spent, I was resigned to keeping my experience to myself, maybe tell Tom privately because he was the only one who would really appreciate the importance of what I had seen. Besides, who could follow Hank?

Unfortunately, I could.

It was Dr. Shlecter's idea, not mine. He broke into the euphoria of Hank's epiphany with, "This has been quite a day, and there's more. Bill has something he wants to share."

I knew to share anything but, "I love you, Hank," followed by a chorus of Bi-Coastal would be a mistake. The guy had only been publicly gay for 40 minutes and he was loving it.. God knows what was waiting for him in the outside world, but in that room he had ten more minutes of total acceptance and I didn't want to take those away from him. Also, there's an old show business adage about following a great act: "I wouldn't give that spot to a leopard." Dr. Shlecter was determined to give it to me.

In retrospect, I think Shlecter set me up in retaliation for refusing to pay for the appointment I missed. The one thing most therapists share, regardless of their training, is the conviction that what you get from therapy is directly related to paying for it, no excuses accepted (interesting to note hookers operate on the same principle). I begged off one final time, but then, in the words of Michael Corleone: "Just when I thought I was out, he dragged me back in…"

"Bill, we're in a zone of openness, the group is bonding, go with the energy."

So, I went…and I almost never came back.

I started with the obligatory tribute to Hank, his courage and dignity. Then, realizing there was no way out, took my best shot: "For the past six weeks, we've been dealing with our personal quest for understanding and fulfillment and, so far, only Hank has come to the end of the road." I realized that was an unfortunate choice of words, so immediately added, "and the beginning to his new path, his *true* path! And we all wish him Godspeed.

"What I have been seeking pales in comparison, but let's look again. Why is the search for love and romance any less meaningful than to discover you're gay? Actually, isn't that what Hank has been searching for? Only now he knows where to start looking. It seemed the more I tried to elevate my discovery, the lower I pushed Hank.

"Look, guys, I know that every time I talk about the kind of magic I want, you all roll your eyes to Heaven, like: 'Here he goes again.' Bernie told me I've seen too many movies and that life isn't like that. Tom, in his pain, knows life *can* be like that: he had it and lost it." Tom moaned. "Well, I'm here to tell you, it isn't just in the movies! It *exists* because I saw it just the other night, and it was everything Tom had ever lived and I had ever hoped for!" The mood was changing. I had them. Even Shlecter leaned forward wanting more.

"Last week was tough. The ratings were down on my show. I was at the studio late every night trying to fix things. All I wanted was to go home and have her waiting, excited to see me, looking great just to let me know I mattered. I buttoned up against the chill night air and the emptiness I felt inside." Heads nodded in recognition.

"It was a full moon, crystal clear, you could see your breath hanging in the air. In the distance, I imagined hearing Barry White singing, 'Can't get enough of your love, babe.' As I approached the guard at the gate, the music got louder, and suddenly, a white Jaguar convertible came screaming around the corner, top down, music blaring, with this beautiful creature at the wheel, black hair flying, like ebony flames." They were eating it up.

"She waved to the guard, and, in one motion, screeched to a stop, was out of the car, running toward a sound stage at the end of the studio street. It was Nancy Kwan, the actress." I noticed a sudden shift in attention and started to embellish.

"As if she weren't already a vision beyond imagination, she was wearing a white fur coat that seemed to make love to her as she moved. Everything felt as if it was in slow motion, and I just wanted, for one moment, to be whomever it was she was running to. Whoever it was, you could feel the passion with every step." There was a palpable change in the emotion of the room. Looks of wonder were turning darker with my every word. I was losing them and pushed to get them back.

"At the end of the street, the huge studio doors of the *I Spy* stage slowly parted and a lone figure emerged, shrouded in a swirling mist, the moonlight reflecting from droplets of water on his bare chest." Tom moaned and put his head in his hands; at least I was getting through to *him*. I forged on. "It was Bob Culp, Nancy's new lover, in such a rush to embrace her, he was still wet and shirtless from his shower." Tom gave off an unearthly moan and the others stared at me with a mixture of hatred and disbelief. They just weren't getting it.

I took one last shot. "They hungered to touch one another. The moon, like a spotlight, held only them. Barry White was singing only for them. Finally, they touched and became one."

Suddenly, I was on the floor, with Bernie and Fred on top of me. The room had exploded into screams and curses all directed at me, as Tom lay in a fetal position on the floor next to me. Everyone was screaming and punching at once, including Shlecter.

"You son of a bitch, you bastard, you pervert!" This from Hank, who also scratched me. "How could you do that to him? You know how he loved her!"

I fought my way up. "Do *what* to *whom?* Who loved who?"

"Tom loves Nancy!"

I was lost. "Tom loves Nancy who?"

"Nancy Kwan."

I repeated it in disbelief: "Tom loves Nancy...?"

A violent retch from Tom as Fred grabbed me. "Why do you keep saying it?"

I was trying to make sense of it all. "Because I can't believe it!

A series of retches.

"I'm sorry."

"Sorry's not going to do it, you Bastard!" Fred was particularly hostile. "How could you even mention her name after the way he broke down about her last week?"

I laughed in relief and they started toward me. "Wait, hold it! I wasn't *here* last week!"

They stopped. "You weren't?"

Shlecter jumped in: "No, and he's not planning to pay for it either."

I knelt next to Tom. "I'm sorry. Honest, I didn't know. I never would have told that story if I knew you loved Nancy Kwan." Tom threw up on my shoes.

DOCTOR, HEAL THYSELF

My journey in search of understanding, self-esteem, and happiness has, over the years, included a library of self-help books and a varied selection of therapists, who shall remain nameless to protect them and me, with the exception being Doctor Stephen Rittenberg, for whom I have only appreciation. The rest were pretty much a waste of time, money, energy, and emotion: although there was one observation along the way that made a difference. It came after the 4th appointment with a therapist when I told him it wasn't going to work out; something I knew when he told me to call him Stan. I already knew two Stans, and didn't need another friend. As I was leaving, he said, "I'm not at all worried about you."

I was glad one of us wasn't.

He continued: "You don't realize the most important thing."

I waited expectantly.

"You're tall and you have hair."

It was clear to him that I didn't get it.

"Think about it: you could be short and have hair, or you could be tall and have no hair. Or, how about this? You could be short and have no hair. But you…you have it all."

It may not be Freud, but countless times since, when life wasn't going my way, I'd remind myself to be grateful: I was tall and had hair.

During a later, short venture into therapy, again before I

left, I received another invaluable gift. I was lying there talking about my father, whose complexities would have challenged Freud, Jung, Shakespeare and Dr. Phil. I was recounting a disaster of the previous night when, being his quintessential self, he had turned a minor problem into a full-blown disaster. As I turned to the doctor to emphasize my point, I caught him shaking his head in disbelief.

Knowing he was caught, he said, "I have to admit; he takes the cake." Now there is a "Get Out of Emotional Jail Free card; of all the difficult fathers he had heard about, mine took the cake!

My shortest psychiatric adventure lasted exactly 27 minutes: it was called "primal pain reduction" and practiced by Darryl, an actor who had once played a psychiatrist on a soap opera, had been to EST twice, and had done LSD with Timothy Leary. With credentials like that, how could you resist?

Actually, I tried to, but since my marriage was crumbling and my wife said he could save it, I was willing to try anything.

She had met him at a three-day juice fast where they had both gotten high on emptiness and he touched her inner eye. The weird thing is that at the time in L.A., it didn't seem weird.

I knew I was in trouble when I got to his office, which was his apartment on the second story of a two-family house (just in passing, therapy in apartments, houses, and mobile homes doesn't work). I rang the bell and a disheveled child of about six answered— another harbinger of the bizarre experience to come. The smell of incense was overpowering but couldn't cover the telltale aroma of pot roast coming from the kitchen. A baby was crying in another room and the place was a mess with no place to sit, so I just stood there trying to decide if saving my marriage was really that important.

I had pretty much decided it wasn't when the closed

door opened and Darryl emerged. To say he *entered* the room just wouldn't capture it. He was bathed in a cloud of incense, dressed in a flowing robe, a turban, carrying either the crying baby or his inner child—at this point I wasn't ruling anything out.

He greeted me with some kind of *Star Trek* salute and called out, "Suphed," which I took as a form of blessing, but turned out to be the name of his wife who came in from the kitchen, looking like a normal person but with a definite stunned look in her eyes. She took the baby, bowed to him (O.K., forget the normal part), and left. He went into the other room and indicated I should follow. I thought about making a break for it but decided to see it through.

The room was a combination shrine/nursery, which explained why the baby was crying; it probably thought it was going to be sacrificed. Darryl sat on the floor and I had a choice of joining him or getting into the crib, which, based on what followed, wouldn't have been a bad idea.

He started by saying he knew a lot about me from what he had seen through my wife's inner eye. Apparently, it wasn't good because he felt we would have to commit to a long journey together, but only after I went home and performed a cleansing ritual.

I was all for the going home part but told him I couldn't agree to the cleansing thing until I knew more about it.

As he started to explain, his voice and manner became semi-religious. I knew I was in trouble—again—when he asked if we had a baby bottle.

I said we didn't, and he reached into a cabinet filled with them and gave me one. I sat there holding the bottle and my breath through the following:

I was to go home and have my wife draw me a warm bath and heat some warm milk for the bottle (so far, that would be more than she had done for me in the five years we had been married), then, after my bath, she was to dry me with a warm towel and hold me in her arms, feeding me the bottle while I masturbated.

I exploded into gales of uncontrollable laughter as much for the image of it all as its absurdity. Darryl sat patiently waiting for me to stop, and when I did, said in a gentle but superior manner, "Laugh if you will, but the first time I did it, I cried for three hours."

I managed to stifle my laughter, paid him $50, but kept the bottle as a reminder of the fine line between therapy and insanity. I don't know what happened to Darryl, but I have a feeling he went on to treat Charles Manson and Jeffrey Dahmer.

In the end, with Dr. Rittenberg's help, I managed to free my foot for a kick in the ass and it got me moving in a happier direction.

I guess the thing to remember about most therapists is that many of them started the study of psychology to get a better understanding of themselves and you have to be lucky to get one who actually succeeded.

   ***

A few months later, my life changed dramatically, or, in my case, comedically, with the introduction of two very important women. The first I'll call Ingred, because that was actually her name, and I couldn't think of a better one. The whole thing was fairly harmless, and although a major event in my life, I doubt she would remember it…or me.

IT HAPPENED IN TAHITI

That sounds like an Elvis Presley movie. In fact, I think it was.

I went there in 1969 to produce a television pilot called, *Three for Tahiti*, based on three Americans who had gone there in the early 60s, fallen in love with the place, and— judging from the countless blond Tahitian children running around—most of the women on the island. We shot and lived at the Bali Hai, the bamboo and palm frond hotel they had built.

My two weeks there, even pre-Ingred, changed my view of life, myself, and just about everything else. There was just something in the air, the light, and the people that made you realize joy and happiness are part of nature and you can have your share without depriving anyone else of theirs.

It was a completely different experience from my survey trip a few weeks earlier with my wife Linda. She'd hated it: the flight, leaving L.A. at midnight and arriving ten hours later in Papeete where we spent two hours waiting for an inter-island flight, drinking strong French coffee in the seedy airport bar heavy with the smoke of a thousand Galois smoked by a dozen versions of Peter Lorre and Sidney Greenstreet, then the vintage plane and a death-defying flight to the island of Moorea and the hotel. She'd hated that, too, and the three guys – whom she felt were boorish and exploiting the natives. By the time we'd left, I dreaded the thought that I had to come back. I have a feeling that if Gauguin had taken his wife along, there would have been a lot fewer paintings in The Louvre.

So, two weeks later, I boarded the midnight flight for my return to Tahiti with a heavy heart…which was quickly lightened by the arrival of my seat partner, Laolani, a majestic 80-year-old beauty who happened to be a Tahitian princess. In her honor, the champagne and caviar started flowing and the party that was to be my life for the next two weeks had begun. The ten-hour flight that had been a chore was now an adventure; the wait at the airport bar was a smoke-filled wonderland as Laolani added brandy to my coffee and had all the Lorres and Greenstreets singing Tahitian songs and dancing the Tamure. I'm sure the flight to Moorea was still death-defying, but I couldn't be certain because apparently I had one brandied coffee too many and woke up in my hut at the Bali Hai several hours later. I tentatively opened my eyes and saw a giant lizard clinging to the thatched roof above just as he welcomed me to the island by shitting on my head.

Life was good! And got better every day!

The series never got on the air, which was O.K. given that selling it was secondary to the experience of doing it. The whole island was ours, and the natives, who love a party, kept ours going from sunrise to sunrise. We worked too hard, slept too little, danced and drank too much, but were never tired, nor did we ever lose sight of the fact that we were part of a very special experience. To this day, some 50 years later, when I come across anyone who was part of that project there is a warm smile and a gentle nod of recognition for the magical time we shared.

As if the whole thing weren't already perfect, on the eighth day, *she* arrived: Ingred—blonde, beautiful—an airline stewardess when they were still objects of fantasy. She flew for Pan Am from San Francisco, and always spent her layover at the

Bali Hai. She arrived about 9 a.m. and by 10:30, I was in love. She told Kelly, one of the three guys, that she thought I was cute. Nobody who looked like her had said that about me for a long time...if ever. It would have felt good hearing that anywhere, but underneath a palm tree with a cold beer? Irresistible.

Ingred stopped to watch as we were shooting a scene, and I tried to look absorbed in my work, yet approachable. When we finished, Kelly introduced us and I said, "Hello." I was trying to convey that I was a caring, sensitive, strong, talented, funny, successful, charming, interesting person. Before I could further impress her with my coolness, my friend Bob Hogan, who was starring in the show, wanted to discuss something in the script so I excused myself with a look that said, "Business before pleasure, duty calls," and quickly said, "Nice to meet you," managing to convey all the character traits of the Boy Scout oath.

Because the show was the major event on the island, she, along with everyone else, hung around to watch and during the breaks drink beer, swim, dance, and sing our new repertoire of Tahitian songs. By the end of the day, we seemed to be doing all those things together and if there was a step up from Paradise, I was on it. A great-looking, bright, worldly woman thought *I* was something special and I began to think so myself.

The big scene of the show was a luau to celebrate the completion of the hotel. By nightfall, every man, woman, child, cat, dog, and goat had assembled to be in it: easily 2,000 people plus sundry domesticated fauna. In Hollywood, it would've cost a million dollars; in Tahiti, all the beer you could drink and all the roasted pig, poi, papaya and mangos you could eat. We started at eight and finished at three in the morning, but the party and the music hadn't slowed or quieted when Ingred and I went to sit on the beach and watch the sun come up before she left to work her return flight to San Francisco.

As much as I hated to see it end, I was glad it did because I avoided the moral dilemma I would have faced had she been able to stay. This way was perfect: no guilt or recriminations, just a joyous experience and a sense of new possibilities for my life.

I knew I wanted to see her again, or at least talk to her, so I asked for her phone number. There was nothing to write with, but I told her I would remember and I do to this day: 415-776-0996. How I remember is so pathetic that I'm almost embarrassed to reveal it, but it's who I was at the time, and in a way, it was kind of poetic.

As she finished saying, "776-0996," I immediately responded: "How can I forget? '776' is for 1776 when independence was declared; '0' is for Oh, how good it feels; '99' is two people lying together, and '6' is for how sick I am that we can't."

She was stunned – either by my absurdity or brilliance – then, not wanting to find out which, without another word, we embraced and I walked off into the sunrise. Her last image of me was diving gracefully into a breaking wave in water so shallow I cut my nose and scraped my chest on coral, but she never knew that.

To make the whole thing seem like the ending of a romance novel, later that morning her plane flew low over the island on its way to San Francisco and I could swear it dipped its wings as I heard "Leaving on a Jet Plane" playing softly in my mind.

Of course it was all a fantasy and not really about Ingred, as delightful as she was. What stayed real was how I felt about myself for that perfect moment in time, and the awareness that there could be more moments like those.

My flight home was like Alice coming back through the looking glass: I was returning to reality, but what I had seen and felt gave me a new perspective and though I didn't know what to do with it, I wanted it to last. Obviously, that glimpse was connected to Ingred and the minute we landed I would go to a phone booth and dial 415-776-0996. I thought of what to say, from a subtle "Hi," which might not be enough for her to recognize my voice, to: "I hope you were longing to hear my voice as I was to hear yours"—too studied, too stupid and "longing" is a bad word for a guy. It was looming as the most important phone call of my life and I actually wrote a song about it:

Put in 85 cents
And I get three minutes
To tell you how much I miss you
Three quarters and a dime
Won't give me the time
To tell you how much I want to kiss you.

This ain't "the next best thing to being there"*
This ain't the next best thing at all
I can't see your blue eyes and golden hair
Or breathe in your sweet fragrance on a call
*Phone company ad campaign in the 70s.

Country music was deprived of a big hit because the plane landed before the second verse and I was the first one off. My run down the jet way came to an abrupt halt when I saw her standing there, waiting for me: Linda, who, in 14 years, had never come to pick me up at the airport.

Why now? Did she know?

It never dawned on me that she had actually missed me, which opened the floodgates of guilt because I hadn't missed her . On the ride home it was clear that she had missed my presence more than my person as she detailed all she had been through in my absence. Gradually, Tahiti slipped away, and with it any sense of the possibilities the island had awakened.

A few days later I started editing the show, and as the film ran through the Moviola, as I saw the beauty of the island and heard the music, the joy of my time there began to feel very real again. That night, on my way home, every phone booth seemed to beckon until I found myself "putting in 85 cents" and dialing, not knowing what to expect or what to say. I never realized the word "Hello" could be so powerful until she said it.

My heart was racing. I didn't know whether to answer or run. Finally, I managed, "It's me," and her response was all I could have hoped for: "It's about time."

We talked until I ran out of change, and every day over the next few weeks when she was home.

My phone affair made me realize I wanted my life to change and that the change had to start with my marriage—not by divorce, but by dealing with how to make everything better for both of us.

It seemed that every attempt at talking matters out became a restatement of blame and re-fortifying of defenses, making everything worse. I would have gladly gone into therapy, but since I had already been going for two years, therapy wasn't an option.

Meanwhile, the phone calls were losing their luster, more for her than for me, and it was time to either see one another or stop. Although I didn't really have her, I didn't want to lose her and agreed to come to San Francisco. I had a small window of opportunity on Thursday nights when my wife went to her acting class. It started at six and ran until midnight, which would give me an hour to fly up, three hours with Ingred, and an hour to get home.

It was the most out-of-character thing I had ever contemplated. By Thursday, the anxiety was so intense I couldn't breathe, but I kept trying to act normal in abnormal ways: talking incessantly, laying out my day minute-by-minute and creating an intricate alibi for my every move that evening to put me above suspicion which wouldn't have existed if I would just shut up.

Before leaving for the airport, I went home, wished my wife luck at her class, which made no sense, put the kids to bed two hours early, made sure the housekeeper was healthy and in place for the evening and drove to the airport under the speed limit, sure that every police car I passed was going to pull me over for the no-good cheating bastard I was.

Actually, I'd only have about two hours between flights which didn't allow for anything more than dinner at the airport, but in my heart I knew: a martini and a shrimp cocktail were just as damning as a motel room. Like Kenny Rogers' Ruby, "I was taking my love to town," and I didn't feel it was right. If the marriage was over, it should end as clean as possible and not with any dishonesty. Everyone in the airport knew exactly what I was up to, including the ticket agent who commented with a smirk: "Coming back tonight, Mr. Persky?" I covered with a detailed story of a family friend in trouble. I was going up to see if I could help. Her headshake indicated that she didn't buy it, so I went into greater detail: "He needs money to pay a gambling debt, to the mafia, and he's desperate, so I'm bringing him the cash." I stopped short of asking whether she wanted to see the money.

I'm not good at this elaborate deception and in the half-hour before my flight thought of a hundred reasons not to go. When I called home to make sure the kids were O.K., I found one: the housekeeper asked where I'd be because I'd forgotten to leave a number.

That did it. What if something—and I thought of a million possibilities— happened to my kids and I wasn't reachable? It wasn't about guilt, but the sudden awareness of how irresponsible the whole thing was. My romance was over.

I cashed in my ticket and had no need to explain when the agent looked at me questioningly. There was nothing to hide. I was just a guy going home to his kids. I stopped in a phone booth and dialed 776-0996 for the last time as my plane took off into a crimson sunset. As if on cue, the song coming over the airport music system was Frank Sinatra singing: "My Way."

***

The second woman I'll call Holly because the name suggests Christmas and good times, which suits her, and though our meeting took place by chance and went no further than conversation, that meeting played a part in ending my marriage.

About two months after Ingred went into the sunset, it was time to deliver the Tahiti show to the network in New York. It was to be a quick trip, leaving L.A. on Thursday, the network on Friday, and home on Friday night. But then my presentation was delayed until too late to make the last flight and I had to stay the night.

I called an old friend to see if we could get together for dinner, which we did, then I tagged along to a party celebrating the divorce of Holly, a model he knew. Her apartment was filled with loud music, no place to stand or sit, crowded with no one I knew, so I was on my way out. Before I was all the way in, I said goodnight to my friend just as she came over.

It was her party and I immediately understood why she had gotten divorced: whoever he was, he wasn't good enough. It's not just the way she looked, which would have been enough, but her spirit and style were irresistible.

We were introduced. I wished her luck in her new life and was about to leave when she invited me to join her and a few friends at P.J. Clarke's, a great hangout on the East Side.

The conversation was about things the group had shared

and people I didn't know, so I quickly finished my drink and was about to leave when, in a quiet moment, someone asked me why I was in New York. I explained about the show.

Holly had been thinking of going to Tahiti as part of her post-divorce rehab program, so she moved next to me to find out more. She understood everything I felt about it, savoring every detail of the people and the music. After we had exhausted that topic, we went on to countless others, and, when I dropped her off about 3:30 a.m., it was as if we hadn't even started.

There was a moment when I was close to going up to her apartment, but we agreed she was too fresh out of her marriage and I was still in mine, so we let it go. That was it, except for a gentle hug and the feeling of being appreciated, which was so missing in my life.

THE FINAL CURTAIN

For a long while, it was clear to both Linda and me that we were not happy and something had to change. My suggestion was couple's therapy; hers was for me to join her acting class—a pseudo Actor's Studio/group therapy/EST/New Age-type workshop—and get some insight from Milo, her teacher-guru, and here I should add the titles of Hustler and Fraud.

I'm trying not to editorialize, but facts are facts. Milo was an out-of-work actor who once stood in the doorway of the Actor's Studio during a thunderstorm and came away convinced he was the next Lee Strasberg by way of Carl Jung. Somehow he managed to convince 30 aspiring actors, including my wife, that he was the answer to stardom through "Becoming one with their inner truth." At $50 a class, he had a great thing going, especially with eight beautiful young aspirants who came to him and were told in his "evaluation" that they had no sexuality.

In my evaluation, they had enough to star in every porn film ever made.

Milo kept berating them until in a "private session" he would suddenly announce that they had had a breakthrough and proved it by having sex with them, which somehow or another was supposed to bring them one step closer to stardom.

Against every instinct, in my effort to go the extra mile I signed up. She was in the Tuesday "advanced" class while I was relegated to the Thursday night "beginners" and from the first session it was clear Milo and I weren't going to get along.

He sat in a chair with the students—supplicants, really—at his feet, but because of my bad back I needed a chair, which put me on a level with him. Even more upsetting, I was a successful writer/producer who represented potential work: my classmates started to ask *me* questions rather than *him*.

Milo reported to my wife that unless I turned myself over to the experience and let go of the need for control, I couldn't get in touch with the part of me that needed to open up. I promised to give it my best shot, which is what I felt like taking at Milo.

Over the next two weeks, he tried to regain the upper hand by calling on me to do things that were "risky" (stupid) in hopes that I would either refuse or make a fool of myself in the attempt. I did neither, giving up control and doing whatever he threw at me.

Actually, it was kind of fun: making believe I desperately needed to pee and being unable to find a bathroom; being a baby coming through the birth canal; taking a quick look around after emerging and deciding to go back (to uproarious laughter and applause). By the third week, I was the star of the class, and, although things weren't better at home, she had to admit I was trying.

Probably the best thing to come out of the class, other than the realization that our marriage was over, was my friendship with Alex Rocco who went on play Moe Green in *The Godfather* (he's the casino operator who gets shot in the eye), which was his first step in a great career. We became instant friends. When he came to our house for dinner, she decided she wanted to come to our class and do a scene with him, which both he and I found awkward, made even more so by the fact that she picked something I had written.

The piece was for a television special I was about to direct, "The First Nine Months Are the Hardest," starring Sonny & Cher, based on our experiences during my wife's pregnancy with Dana. The scene was set in the final days of pregnancy when you just can't wait for the whole thing to be over: she is tired of being fat and uncomfortable, and he is tired of being supportive. It was wonderfully warm and funny, which under Milo's direction turned into a combination of Virginia Woolf meets Medea.

During the discussion that followed about "inner truth" subtext and the author's intent, I had finally had it with the insanity of it all, and said, "*I* am the author, and my intent was to get laughs!" something Milo's inner truth seemed to miss.

It was the moment of truth—inner and otherwise—between us and he responded by asking if I would be willing to do an improvisation of the scene with my wife. I figured things couldn't get any weirder, so why not?

He wanted a moment to give her a "subtext" to play, something she had learned in her private sessions. I went up on the stage as the two of them went through what appeared to be an agonizing exchange, hardly the stuff comedy is built on.

The scene started with the husband reading the paper, so while they agonized I started to read. Her first line was, "Am I fat?" and his response: "Compared to what?" When she finally made her entrance and said her line, I looked up, and the anger on her face was so powerful I couldn't speak. Whatever Milo had learned in private was right there on the stage with 30 people watching.

I knew something serious was going on and almost stopped it, but decided to see where it went. Where it went was progressively worse as I kept trying to diffuse the situation by getting back to the comedy as she grew increasingly angry. I have to admit, the whole episode was actually a pretty powerful experience and the audience didn't know whether to laugh, cry, or run for cover.

The scene ended to huge applause as Milo proudly started to expound on the inner truth we had reached, and I had to agree. Until that moment, with all of the fights and discussions, I'd never realized how unhappy and angry she was.

Milo took it as a compliment, that what his class had experienced was proof, that great acting relies on releasing your inner truth. I interrupted, saying they hadn't experienced acting but the end of our marriage and that Milo was a dangerous and irresponsible fraud who shouldn't be trusted with their secrets, their careers, or their lives.

Everyone was in shock (especially poor Alex, who to this day thinks he caused our divorce). Dramatically, I jumped off the stage – fortunately not landing on my face – and left the theater. The scene was followed by a sleepless night of rehashing, which made it clear that the only reason for me to stay on was to be included in John Kennedy's book, *Profiles in Courage.*

The next morning was painful but I was surprisingly calm, packing a few of the essentials to get me through the next few days. Fortunately, Dana, who was eight, had left for six weeks of camp the day before and we saw no need to ruin her adventure by telling her, so that painful conversation was put off. The twins were only three and would hardly understand, so I made them breakfast as always and left as if I was going to work, drove down the hill to the waiting arms of the Fountain View West , L.A.'s halfway house on the road to divorce in the early 70s. I had called Ted Bessel, who played Don Hollinger, the boyfriend in *That Girl,* and who had told me his apartment was available whenever I needed it. He had left the key for me before leaving for the day's shooting.

I had known for some time my marriage was over and

every time I approached the Fountain View on my way home from work, its V-shaped entrance morphed into a pair of arms reaching out to welcome me. It also had the advantage of being just down the hill from "our" house so when I called the kids they could see me standing on the balcony of my apartment. I had already bought them binoculars so it wasn't a case of if, but when.

I finally arrived on a Friday morning in June 1970, still amazingly calm until I went up and started to unpack my essentials, which turned out to be one pair of pants, two shirts, eight pairs of socks, no underwear, and my tuxedo.

THE FOUNTAIN VIEW WEST

Though my memory is fading with time, I will never forget Halloween 1970 and Bethany, a $2000 a night hooker dressed as Snow White dispensing M&Ms to my kids, (though I don't recall if she was dressed for the holiday or her next client). As bizarre as it sounds, it was actually just an ordinary night at The Fountain View, a 12-story building with 50 apartments, each with a tale of its own. The occupants were either newly separated husbands, mostly in show business, or high-priced hookers hoping to get into show business, as well as a few mistresses. The combination made for some great conversations at the free continental breakfast: the guys on their way to a day's work, the girls returning from a night's. Although some very meaningful and emotionally helpful relationships were formed, the unwritten law was: No Sex Among the Occupants. (That would upset the balance of camaraderie.)

Only two exceptions were allowed: one of the guys had an affair with the mistress of a network executive we all hated, meaning we were finally screwing him. The other exception was the wedding of two people who, as of this writing, are still together.

After some efforts at reconciliation in my marriage, which became increasingly hostile confrontations, it was clear that we no longer belonged together and probably never had. When our daughters run into people who have met us both and who say they can't imagine that we were ever married, Jamie and Liza say:

"We can't imagine they were ever in the same elevator together."

After about three weeks it was time to leave Teddy's apartment for one of my own. Because they were all identical, right down to the bedside lamps—a replica of a cavalry boot with a shade depicting a battle from the French Revolution—the only thing that changed was my number and my mood because now I was officially out.

As I went through the supermarket on my first shopping spree, I realized it was something I should do with my daughters to let them feel part of "daddy's new house". We had a wild, sugar-filled shopping spree and after a dinner that would have cost me custody (hot dogs, pizza, Häagen Dazs butter pecan, M&Ms, Häagen Dazs chocolate chip, Oreos, and a night cap of Breyers Cherry Vanilla) the kids slept over.

I can't say anyone was happy with the new world in which we found ourselves, but I wanted to make it as safe and painless for them as I could. They liked the apartment: especially the fact that you could see my terrace from the windows of their bedrooms and with the binoculars I had bought them they could see me when we talked on the phone, which amounted to 22 calls a day. They especially liked it when I hung from the awning rail and acted like a chimp.

The next night I was in a hopeful but melancholy mood as Teddy and I mused on the vagaries of life, love, and the meaning of it all. He assured me "it all" would become much clearer if we smoked a joint. Considering the number of firsts I'd experienced in recent weeks, I figured it was time to take this next step into "The New Me" . But the "Old Me" was still in charge and I took my first step into the drug culture with anything but a true sense of adventure and absolutely no abandon. Teddy lit up, took a deep drag, and before he could offer it to me, I was busy making preparations.

I knew marijuana made you hungry and I decided I would want spaghetti. I had no desire for Italian food at that moment but was sure that when I was in the throes of drug-induced cravings they would be for pasta. I started to fill a pot with water as Teddy suggested I should be a little more spontaneous about the whole thing. I assured him I was and that I would definitely want spaghetti and should have it ready since I didn't want to be dealing with an open flame once I was stoned.

I started to make a meat sauce from scratch but he convinced me that with grass, ketchup would taste just as good. I sat down, took the joint, and just as I was about to take a drag, I panicked.

What was I thinking?! We were on the 12th floor and the terrace door was wide open! What if I got disoriented or suicidal? Luckily I had spotted the open door before I lost control. After locking the door and closing the drapes to give Teddy more time to intercept me if I moved in that direction, I made a final check of the spaghetti water, which was ready, and so, finally, was I.

Since I was a smoker, the inhaling was not a problem. I took my first drag, held it, and was pleased to note my voice had that funny sound people in the movies make while they are toking. I exhaled and waited—for what I wasn't sure—but nothing seemed to happen. Teddy assured me it took time and I should just relax. A minute, two, three, and still nothing, so I took another deep inhale and held it even longer. Again, I waited, and nothing. After a third, I was convinced I was immune: no buzz, no visual distortion, no giggles, no mad desire for spaghetti, nothing. Nothing but the fact that the Beatles, on the *Abbey Road* album cover I was looking at, seemed to have changed places. Paul, who had been in front, was now last, Ringo was second, then he moved to third, and John was second. I closed my eyes and when I opened them the Beatles were all moving again. Then came the laughing, the brilliant epiphanies, insights, clarity, and finally the spaghetti with the most incredible sauce I had ever tasted.

As the weeks went by, I fell into a routine of concentrating on work and making sure the girls were O.K. I knew I would have to expand into dating, but wasn't looking forward to it and didn't know how, then one day at the office my phone rang and I didn't have to think about it anymore: It was Holly, the girl I had met in New York.

She was in town and wondered if we could have a drink. I told her I had left my wife and we could have whatever we wanted. I went by, put the girls to bed, and met Holly for a drink.

One year later we were married.

Life with Holly was special – as she was and is today – and was always filled with adventure, surprises and even in difficult times, a lot of laughs, mostly at ourselves.

THE DRESS

In 1974, having sworn off ever going back to Mexico again, Holly and I were offered a free vacation at Tres Vidas en La Playa, a private club just completed by three billionaires who had fallen in love with 2,000 acres of oceanfront outside of Acapulco and who had decided to pool their loose change to build the most extravagant resort in the world. Nothing good had ever happened to me in Mexico unless you count hepatitis, amoebic dysentery, robbery, and a scorpion bite, but from what I had heard and seen in magazines, Tres Vida was going to change my luck.

Guests were housed in their own villas overlooking the ocean across an orchid-filled pool. The floors were mahogany, the walls hand-crafted tiles, and the furniture specially designed by Giorgio Armani. The bathrooms had sterling silver and gold fixtures and the beds were dressed in Porthault linens changed daily by your personal maid. The grounds were covered with thousands of flowers and trees, with almost as many gardeners to tend them, golf on two championship-caliber golf courses, every facility you could imagine and some you couldn't. The kitchen was open 24 hours a day to serve any food known to humans, prepared by the five-star chef the trio had stolen from Maxim's in Paris. The place made present-day Dubai look like a slum.

So, whatever Montezuma's next revenge awaited me, Holly and I couldn't resist the invitation from a wealthy acquaintance who loved *The Dick Van Dyke Show* and who had an unquenchable thirst for inside stories. Based on the rates at Tres Vedas, our week there would cost him more to hear the tales than I made in three years of living them.

Holly was thrilled until she read an article about the club in *Vogue* featuring photographs of women guests in their designer dresses, pants, shorts, bikinis and robes. She went into wardrobe hysteria: suddenly, nothing in her closet or any store in L.A. seemed appropriate.

As anxiety replaced anticipation, she went about putting together an impressive array of outfits but was still missing that one knockout item: something so special, *Vogue* would come back just to see her in it. The day before we left, she found it -- an elegant, long, flowing, white cotton dress with delicate embroidery at the neck. She modeled it for me—she looked sensational—and the next morning we left on our journey into opulence.

It started at the airport where we were greeted by a liveried chauffer who delivered us to the club in a white Rolls Royce convertible. We rode for about a mile on a road bordered by a 15-foot high wall surrounding the entire property. The entrance was impressive with enormous hand-wrought iron gates and a small army of heavily-armed guards. Clearly, at Tres Vidas you were either invited or dead.

Once through the gates, it was as if we had been transported to another plane of existence where everything was perfect. Before you could think of something you wanted, somebody had already brought it to you.

Nothing—including the weather—was less than spectacular, with the exception of the mixed feelings of discomfort in the midst of all this decadence as hundreds of underpaid Mexican workers scurried in all directions to accommodate the excess, along with the armed guards for protection. It seemed as if all the rich people in the world— which didn't include us—were suddenly in the same place. Everywhere you went was like a walk on the red carpet at the Oscars with beautiful women dressed in the perfect outfit for the occasion.

For five days, Holly held her own and hadn't yet found a need to un-leash "The Dress." She was saving it for something special, but since everything that happened there was special, I couldn't imagine what she had in mind.

It came in the form of an invitation to a reception and dinner that evening for the opening of The Princess Hotel, the newest, biggest, and most luxurious—second to Tres Vidas— addition to the Acapulco Riviera. It was the social event of the season and everyone at The Club was invited.

There was a flurry of shopping that afternoon as most of the women went into Acapulco to find something special for the occasion but we just enjoyed the day knowing Holly was set. When it was time to leave for the big event, she came out of the bedroom looking sensational in "The Dress," set off by a white orchid from the pool in her hair. She was going to sweep into The Princess like old royalty, and I could anticipate the gasps as she made her entrance.

Actually, her entrance went unnoticed since there were 50 waitresses wearing the exact same dress and flower. After a moment of shock, we laughed at the absurdity of the whole experience, which was topped off when the maitre d' came over and told her to stop standing around and go take a drink order from table 20. She probably would have done it if I hadn't stopped her. As I said, Holly was special.

SIX WEEKS WITH
ORSON WELLES

Sam and I had written an updated version of the George S. Kaufman/Moss Hart play *The Man Who Came to Dinner* for the *Hallmark Hall of Fame* and it was agreed that Orson Welles was the only one who could play the lead, but he couldn't play it in America: he owed so much in back taxes to the IRS he couldn't work in the U.S. and keep any of the money. As a result, he lived an elegant expatriate life with an apartment in London and open invitations to all the best villas, palaces, and estates of Europe, living off the legend he was and the charmer he remained. Whatever unhappiness this caused Mr. Welles, it led to one of the most joyous experiences of my career, if not my life. We were off to London. It couldn't have come at a better time personally, given that Holly and I were going through a difficult time. She very much wanted a baby, but I was so overwhelmed by the problems dealing with my own kids I just couldn't consider having another one. The trip was a great way of brushing the problem away.

Always one of the world's great cities, in the 70s it was the trend-setter for the whole Western world, and judging from the hundreds of Saudi princes in Ferraris filled with un-burquad blondes, for the Middle East as well. But for me, if I were going to Siberia to work with Mr. Welles, it would have been fine—London just made it that much better.

We were also the producers and we hired Buzz Kulik to

direct. In addition to being a good director, his credits included the highly acclaimed and Emmy-winning TV movie, *Brian's Song*. Buzz was tough, an ingredient we thought necessary with someone as powerful as Mr. Welles. (I will refer to him as "Mr. Welles" until the point in this recounting of our relationship when he insisted I call him Orson.) Buzz did a brilliant job on the show, but early in the rehearsal period it became clear Welles was going challenge him and Buzz was going to show Orson Welles who was boss. It is my belief that "that" director doesn't exist, including whoever is running things wherever Mr. Welles is spending eternity.

"The Kulik-Welles War" started on the second day of rehearsal with "The Battle of the Cigars". Sheridan Whiteside, the character Mr. Welles was playing, smoked only Hupmann Churchills, a top-of-the-line beauty the size of a small telephone pole that went for $25 per pole. Mr. Welles wanted to use them during rehearsal to help "get the feel of the character," but given that he was going through a box a day, Buzz felt it was an unnecessary expense and refused. Mr. Welles pointed out that, as a director himself, he never considered anything that helped an actor to be unnecessary. This stance led to a heated discussion of directing styles, a listing of credits, and the end of rehearsal as Mr. Welles retired to his dressing room.

It wasn't really the expense as much as the fact that it offered Buzz a convenient place to draw the line, which left us, as the producers, having to erase the line by getting our star what he wanted without undermining our director. We decided that if we could get the cigars (which Mr. Welles wanted) without it costing anything extra (which Buzz wanted), we had a graceful way out.

We got in touch with the Hupmann distributor in London and convinced him that with all the photographers and news crews covering our rehearsals, it would be to Hupmann's advantage to be sure Mr. Welles always had a Churchill in his mouth or hand.

The Hupmann guy agreed but had to check with superiors and would get back to us tomorrow. That left us with today and no cigars. I suggested the representative send a box by messenger as Hupmann's gift to a great star and the messenger would return with my personal check, which would be our secret. The cigars arrived a half hour later, rehearsal continued, and the first battle ended in a draw.

At the end of the day, Mr. Welles' assistant, Miss Cabot, asked me to come to his dressing room. When I arrived, with the anxiety such a summons provoked, Mr. Welles was still in the shower. Miss Cabot knocked hesitantly on the bathroom door, and he boomed out that I should make myself comfortable... not an easy task with Miss Cabot. She was an aloof, elegant, and probably once-beautiful woman in her mid-70s, right out of Jane Austen, who did everything for Mr. Welles, and if called upon, would probably kill. She had been with Mr. Welles—as she still referred to him—for 15 years and no doubt had been in love with him even longer.

Finally, he emerged wrapped in a plush, black terrycloth robe, a Churchill in his mouth, a glass of champagne in his hand, and a presence that took your breath away. He asked if I would like an Irish whiskey and I assured him I would because, coincidentally, that was what I drank. His smile, combining a touch of the devil with innocence, told me it was no coincidence and that nothing escaped him.

As further proof, Miss Cabot handed me my drink and a check for £153, the exact amount I had paid for the cigars. Somehow, he knew everything that had happened, thanked me for how I had handled it, gave me a bear hug and told me to henceforth call him "Orson."

It was a heady moment. As I sipped my drink, the elegant explosion that filled my senses told me this was no ordinary Irish whiskey. Noticing my reaction, he asked if it was satisfactory and I assured him it was fine.

"Fine?" he thundered. "Billy, your mouth has just been blessed with the majestic kiss of 100-year-old Bushmill's and if you can't tell the difference between that and the swill you've been drinking, then by all means let's save it for a more deserving palate!"

From that night on, I was his protector, his friend and confidant. Over the next weeks I came to appreciate fine whiskey, magnificent wines and cigars, but mostly the man himself. With all his excesses, moods, and the mayhem he caused, he was always fascinating, brilliant, mysterious, and exciting. There are many individual moments that bear telling but my weekend in Paris that he arranged—though didn't pay for—as well as the story behind the making of one his greatest films, and most memorable of all, our farewell at midnight in a thick Southampton fog at the end of production will always linger with me.

When he heard Holly wanted to spend a weekend in Paris, his city, he took over completely and it was memorable in that I managed to live through it without the gout, diabetes, or cirrhosis of the liver. He arranged for us to stay at his Paris favorite, l'Hôtel, an elegant but unknown hideaway on the left bank that went on to become a destination of choice for those in the know. Our room was small but the view was vast and with a tray of hors d'oeuvres and bottle of Cristal champagne set on the balcony, we would have been satisfied to never leave.

But Orson had set up a schedule and, after too much to eat and drink, we were picked up by André, his favorite cab driver, for lunch at Ami Louis. The reason he sent André was that if few people had heard of l'Hôtel, nobody but Orson had ever heard of Ami Louis, which today is world-renowned.

Our journey, which started in the very chic Left Bank,

wound its way from boulevards to streets to alleys and things worse than alleys, ended in the parking lot of an abandoned factory. If it weren't for André's personal relationship to Orson, I would have been more prepared to have my throat cut than to be served a meal I will never forget, and still haven't fully digested.

Between the paté at l'Hôtel and Louis' home-made variety, I think I was personally responsible for the demise of half the geese in France. We washed everything down with a bottle of Orson's own private Bordeaux. Then came the duck.

Now any duck is heavy, but *Canard Ami Louis* redefined the category. It was roasted in a nest of paper-thin sliced potatoes that were crisply fried in the dripping duck fat. There is no way you can imagine, or I can describe, how amazing it was. After the first bite I was through, but Louis was just getting started.

There were three more hours of too much wine, cheese, fruit and dessert. The dessert was Chocolate Something that I think was the result of all the chocolate on the planet compressed into a two-inch square. Dessert was followed by brandy and a check for $350, which probably added up to a penny per calorie.

The walk back to the hotel (there was no way to survive sitting in a cab after that meal) took two and a half hours, which got us there with an hour and a half to get ready for the special dinner awaiting us at Chez Denis, a five-star Orson favorite. In preparation, I mixed a bizarre concoction of Fernet Branca - a potent, thick, brown, evil-tasting Italian indigestion remedy – with two Alka-Seltzers. I'll never know if it would have worked because the sight of the bubbling brown mass was enough to make me sick…which it did.

We were beyond eating anything more that night and for the rest of our lives, but it was time for Chez Denis. To cancel would have been an affront to Orson who had managed to get us a reservation—those were usually made at least a month in advance.

The owner, Justine, greeted us with great fanfare as he led us to "His" favorite table. Just passing people eating was a challenge. I ordered a Fernet Branca, minus the Alka-Seltzer, and when Justine came over to explain the menu, we tried to be enthusiastic, but obviously didn't pull it off. He looked at us knowingly and asked, "Still tasting the duck from Ami Louis?"

I responded with a dyspeptic nod and he laughed. "Oh, that Orson! Just because he can do both in one day doesn't mean a normal human being can."

Graciously, he served us a one-bite portions of all of Orson's favorite dishes—which included just about everything on the menu—so I could honestly report how great Chez Denis had been. On Monday, Orson savored my description of each mouthful and I think he enjoyed our trip to Paris even more than we did.

NOT QUITE
GREGORY PECK

One night in London, Holly and I were having dinner at a neighborhood pub adjacent to a man who, though far less imposing than Orson Welles, turned out to be even more amazing.

With his balding head and conservative tweed jacket, shirt, and tie, we decided he was either a professor of a subject nobody cared about or he owned a shop selling something dusty and of little use in the present-day world. As Holly and I discussed the menu and found nothing special, we settled on the fish and chips, at which point our neighbor awkwardly excused himself for eavesdropping and suggested the shepherd's pie for which this pub was famous.

Though I had never eaten shepherd's pie, he was so uncomfortable about intruding I didn't have the heart to reject his suggestion. We thanked him and started a cross-table conversation that led to him joining us. I wasn't far off regarding his occupation: the printing business, specializing in educational texts.

His name was Randal Clement and we didn't learn much more, other than that he was a widower with no children, two Irish setters, and surprisingly, for the quiet and gentle person he seemed, traveled around London on a Harley Davidson hog.

When he heard that I had been a writer on *The Dick Van Dyke Show*, his favorite, the conversation became more about Dick and Mary than Randal and printing. It was as if meeting an actual television writer was the most exciting thing that had ever happened to him!

When the check came, he reached for it, but I insisted that the treat was ours since he had been such pleasant company. He accepted on the condition we join him at his club for a nightcap: "the chaps" would really get a kick out of meeting me. He was hard to resist and I figured it would be interesting to see a proper English gentleman's club.

As he revved up his Harley, he told us to take a cab to The Pathfinders Club and was off before we got the address. We watched him speed away, figuring we'd never find it, but when a cab pulled up and I asked the driver if he knew where it was, he answered, "Indeed, sir, I do," as if I had asked if he knew how to get to Buckingham Palace.

We were expecting to arrive at an old building full of musty furniture and a bunch of very proper English gentlemen telling printing jokes, but a few minutes later we stopped at an elegant Mayfair townhouse that, except for the Harley parked at the curb, could have belonged to Professor Henry Higgins.

Randal had cleared us at the door and, as we were led back to the bar, we approached a wall filled with portraits of English kings and queens spanning the past hundred years, with a bronze plaque beneath each reading, "With the gratitude of the Royal Family and the British Empire." Clearly this place was not a hangout for printers.

As we continued toward the bar, we passed portraits of men in uniform from every war that Errol Flynn, Douglas Fairbanks, Jr., and Richard Burton had ever fought in the movies: there were Bengal Lancers, a hard-charging member of the Light Brigade, Highland Fusiliers at Khartoum, and photographs of commandos, paratroopers, and frogmen from more recent battles, as well as racks of swords, display cases of medals—mostly the

Victoria Cross (sort of the UK version of the U.S. Congressional Medal of Honor), battle-torn flags, and, finally, the very masculine leather and mahogany barroom populated with several imposing men, some in uniform. The only thing that seemed out of place was Randal as he came to greet us.

After being introduced to General "Something," Commander "Somebody," several Sirs and a Duke, we ordered our drinks and sat at a quiet booth in the corner. Holly commented on what an elegant place it was, to which Randal responded, in his typical understated way, "Yes, we like it."

Clearly I had questions, but Randal was not about to volunteer anything, so I asked, "Who are 'we'? I mean them, you…what is a Pathfinder?"

He "harrumphed" a few times, and gradually it came out that they were "Heroes of the Realm." He made it sound as if it was something to be embarrassed about.

With more prodding, he mumbled his way through the fact that Pathfinders were men who went into battle before the main force, clearing the path for the others to follow, destroying fortifications, demolishing bridges and tunnels…"things of that sort".

I looked around the room and could picture all the men present doing "things of that sort", and then at Randal, who, knowing what I was about to ask, changed the subject with a question about Mary Tyler Moore. But I had to know. "Randal, can I ask what *you* did?" Embarrassed again and averting his eyes, he answered, softly, "I blew up the Guns of Navarone."

In shock, I blurted out, "You blew up the Guns of Navarone?????"

"I'm afraid so," he responded, as if I was going to ask him to pay for the damages.

I had seen the movie 10 times and had to know: "Which

one were you?"

With a devilish glint, he said, "I'd like to think I was Gregory Peck"

AN OFF-THE-RECORD
MOMENT WITH ORSON

Although you can find accounts and stories documenting the making of most of Orson Welles' films, he told me one story that isn't generally known and reveals just what a charming scoundrel he was.

In the late 1940s, when the "boy genius" image that had carried him to Hollywood had worn thin, he was constantly scrambling for money to back his ventures. His chief patsy was Jerry B. Cohn, the president of Columbia Pictures, one of the toughest men in Hollywood, but a pushover for Welles.

They had a love/hate relationship and Cohn vowed each time he dealt with Orson would be the last time Orson would get a penny from him. But, in the end, Orson always found a way. By 1945, Hollywood didn't love him but Broadway still did, and somehow Orson managed to raise the money to produce a play. He also managed to spend it before opening night and needed $50,000 fast, but with one day to go he hadn't raised a dime. He had saved Jerry Cohn until the end, hoping not to let Cohn know he was in trouble again.

He was aware of the fact that Cohn was in his office at 6 a.m. L.A. time, which was 9 a.m. in New York, but Orson didn't want to call too early and seem desperate—of course, he was— and Cohn already knew that because everyone who hated Orson had called to share the good news.

Orson made his first call at 1:30 p.m., 10:30 a.m. in Los Angeles. By 4 p.m. he was starting to panic and didn't go to the bathroom without letting everyone know where he was in case the call came. Finally, about 5 p.m., he went out to the box office to see if there was any business and obviously there wasn't: the attendant had dozed off while reading a book.

Orson figured he was dead when the phone rang—it was Cohn. With the guts of a pirate, Orson told Cohn he'd have to call him back because the box office was overwhelmed and he had to come out to help. He threw in an off-stage, "Sorry, we're sold out on Thursday," to a non-existent buyer and went on regaling Cohn with stories of how great the show was doing.

Finally, Cohn told him how happy he was to hear it since there was no chance in hell he would come up with the $50,000 he knew Orson needed. Without missing a beat, Orson said, "Not even if I give you the rights to my next picture?"

After a long pause, Cohn asked what it was and Orson, taking the book from the still-dozing attendant, turned to the cover and told him, "It's called *The Lady from Shanghai*."

Hooked again, Cohn asked, "What's it about?" and Orson reeled him in with, "I'll tell you when I get the money."

Obviously he did, because though he and Cohn are both gone, *The Lady from Shanghai* will live forever.

MY FAREWELL TO
ORSON WELLES

It was like a scene from *The Third Man*; all it lacked was the zither playing hauntingly in the background.

It was the night we finished production of *The Man Who Came to Dinner*, which had been a difficult, tense experience. Things between the star and the director had gone progressively downhill, and our move from the glamour of London to dreary Southampton didn't help. Although it had a great studio, there wasn't a decent hotel or restaurant to be found, even if the perpetual fog lifted. We were there for six depressing days and never saw the sky, let alone the sun.

The war between Buzz Kulik and Orson Welles led to delays, long hours, and an unhappy crew, so with just one shot remaining, everyone was pushing to finish and get to London in time for a good dinner. By 4 p.m., we were calling to make reservations and by 4:15 everything came crashing down: Orson and Buzz were confronting each other over the final shot. The disagreement started out simple but quickly escalated to the battle of egos that had been building from Day One.

Orson was at the doorway of the house about to make his final exit when he got an idea for something he wanted to do as he left and told Buzz to make the shot closer. Buzz wasn't about to be "told" anything and responded from the control room over a loud speaker on the stage that made him sound like God Himself: "Why don't you show me what you want to do and I'll decide whether to make the shot closer."

Everyone knew that wasn't the end but just the beginning and for the next 10 minutes there was an escalating exchange of barbs, challenges, and insults ending with Orson playing his trump card: "I should remind you, Mr. Kulik, you are talking to the director of *Citizen Kane*".

The response was devastating: "A film I always felt was highly overrated, Mr. Welles, and we'll keep this shot as is."

In a very calm voice, Orson said, "Very well, Mr. Kulik. Now all you need is someone to be in it." And with that, he exited the shot, the stage, and for all we knew, Southampton.

We spent the next two hours looking for Orson and convincing Buzz to apologize when, and if, we did. After checking his hotel and every restaurant in town, Miss Cabot—more out of concern for Orson's reputation than our production—told us to check the Southampton Yacht Harbor. It was an ultra-exclusive private club and though Orson wasn't a member, Prince Philip, who she had called earlier, was.

By the time we managed to reach Orson, convince him to return, and wait as he finished his dessert, brandy, and cigar, it was 11:30. That gave us just a half-hour to get the apology and the final shot before midnight and catastrophic overtime charges.

The private apology wasn't accepted; he wanted it over the PA so that everyone could hear it. Somehow, he got his way, we got our shot with a minute to spare that Buzz used to publicly thank everyone by name…with the glaring omission of Orson Welles. It was a sad conclusion for what turned out to be a wonderful show and the mood at the wrap party was more like a wake than a celebration.

Figuring Orson wouldn't make an appearance, I went to his dressing room to say goodbye. The door was open and he was sitting alone, still in his final wardrobe, a black cape with a Persian lamb collar and hat, looking like a deposed monarch. He actually seemed vulnerable, a feeling you would never associate with him and one that was uncomfortable to witness. It was like peeking around the curtain that shielded the Wizard of Oz and finding what was behind all the bluster.

I felt I should apologize but wasn't sure for what so I just stood there staring blankly and then he started to chuckle, which grew to a deep-throated laugh at some private joke, and suddenly he was Orson Welles again.

"Well, Billy, let's be going. We don't want to be late for the party."

As we climbed the three flights to the cafeteria, with him stopping on each landing to catch his breath, he talked of all the final shots and final parties he had been through, the good times and the bad, and how at the end he always had a feeling of immortality. I can't quote him exactly, but in essence he said each project is like living a complete lifetime, from birth through infancy, maturity, fruition, and its end, yet you live on to go through it all again. This part I can quote: "So I have lived many lifetimes, some tumultuous like this, but many more glorious, and, in the end, I have no concern but running out of the chance to live them, however they may go."

With that, we had reached the cafeteria and could hear the celebration, which ceased the moment he entered. He had been difficult throughout and whatever admiration or respect the crew had felt for him was gone when he had walked out.

It was painful to watch as he gave perhaps his best performance of the whole experience: the revered star and legend bestowing his thanks and appreciation to a room full of people who couldn't wait for him to leave. It had to hurt even him but he never for a moment revealed anything but his sense of entitlement and grandeur. After a painful five minutes, he went to the door and said a final goodnight as if all those people were pleading with him to stay but he really couldn't.

I walked him out to the hall where Martin, his fully uniformed chauffer complete with polished boots, was waiting. I started to say goodbye, but he told me to wait because if he didn't pee immediately he would burst.

He went to the men's room door, which was locked, and we followed Martin as he ran to the second floor and then the first with no luck. We walked out into the parking lot, which was shrouded in fog, made all the more eerie from the glow of a light tower in the distance. Everything was deadly silent but for our footsteps echoing and Orson's bellowing his need to pee.

Martin's voice drifted out of the fog: "Over here, sir."

We followed the disembodied sound to discover Martin standing at a section of the ancient Roman wall that runs through Southampton. It was built in 200 BC and is so revered that streets are rerouted so as to not disturb it.

"Perhaps this will do, sir."

A Roman centurion or Druid may have been the first to piss on it but Orson Welles was going to be the next. Since I didn't need to bear witness, I said a quick goodbye and that I would always treasure the experience of working with him. He interrupted the unzipping of his fly long enough to give me a firm embrace and said he expected great things from me. He shook my hand with his left, since his right was busy, and I walked off into the fog, my footsteps echoing.

This would have been the cue for the zither to come in with "The Third Man Theme," but instead, through the fog wafted the thunderous roar of Orson Welles peeing on the 2,000 year old Roman Wall.

I saw him again five years later at an American Film Institute event in his honor. Everyone in Hollywood was there to salute him. He was surrounded by Fred Astaire, Cary Grant, Ingrid Bergman, Sophia Loren, and Alfred Hitchcock. Love him or hate him, you couldn't deny him.

I was standing across the room at the bar watching and enjoying his moment when he looked in my direction. I didn't think he was actually looking at me, or if he was, would recognize or remember me. Then, suddenly, he raised his arms and shouted, "Billy, come give Orson a hug!" I hugged him hello and three days later hugged Holly goodbye. As devastating as the breakup was, typical of our relationship, it too had its laughs.

When we were invited to play tennis at Larry Gelbart's house with the Reiners, Mel Brooks and Anne Bancroft, Tim Conway and Harvey Korman, it was a fun-filled afternoon but I could feel a sense that the end of our marriage, which had been coming for a while, was finally here. We went through an uncomfortable and polite dinner and then it was more painful to avoid it than confront it. Through a lot of tears on both sides, we realized that if not forever but at least for now, she was in "Mid 70's Madness" and needing to have a child: something I really couldn't handle because I had just gotten full custody of Dana, and she was the only child I had room for. There was no anger, just sadness for both of us and I admit I envied her freedom to just go off and deal with her own needs. I finally fell into a fitful sleep at around 3 o'clock and bolted awake with anxiety ten minutes later and spent the next two hours imagining nothing but disaster ahead. By the time she woke I was doubled up in a fetal position, a sniveling mess pleading with her not to go: until suddenly I stopped sniveling, looked at her and asked, "Am I too macho?" We laughed, had coffee and as I stood in the doorway, she drove the 1958 Mercedes convertible that I had bought her three months earlier to make things better, down the hill: just as I knew she would the day I bought it.

COME ON, MAIDENHAIR FERN

In 1975, the government released a study revealing the five leading causes of stress in America:

1. Divorce
2. Career change
3. Financial concerns
4. Moving
5. Health problems

On May 14th, 1975, I had all five plus a couple they hadn't thought of.

I was facing my second divorce while having just gotten custody of my 12-year-old daughter, Dana, after she and her mother couldn't manage to live together, the reasons being unimportant. Simultaneously, Sam and I decided to end our 20-year partnership since we both had things we wanted to do alone: for me it was to become a director, leading to career change. The divorce and career change led to financial problems, which meant I had to move. And the ensuing anxiety, plus two packs of cigarettes a day, took care of my health. Since the government isn't Jewish, it didn't allow for guilt, panic, and despair.

It was the "Me Decade," and I had managed to make a mess out of me and just about everything else. If there had been a commemorative stamp of the 70s, my picture would have been on it. The only plus I had going was the presence of Mrs. Luberta Clift, my housekeeper then, and my friend to this day.

Holly had just moved out to "find herself," another 70s thing, and I found myself on my second Scotch in a house I couldn't afford with no idea of where to go or what to do when I got there. I knew that, sooner or later, I would have to do something to start on the road back. Or forward. Or somewhere other than where I was. My future was a blank page and after a third Scotch, I decided to fill it with a list of what I needed to do to get through the rest of my life.

I started with the obvious:

> *Make sure the kids know that they are loved and safe*
> *Try not to make the same mistakes again*
> *Learn to be alone*
> *Don't expect miracles*
> *Take the high road about why the relationship ended—*
> > *consider this a beginning, not an end*
> *Stop smoking*
> *Trust myself and my instincts (maybe not)*
> *Have another drink*

Several Scotches and a vodka later (I had run out of Scotch), the list took on a life of its own with fantasies, wishes and things I always wanted to do but couldn't find the time or the courage to try:

> *Move to the beach*
> *Win the Iron Man Competition in Hawaii*
> *Get a plant and take care of it*
> *Learn to cook Chinese*
> *Learn to speak Italian*
> *Learn to play a musical instrument*
> *Take flying lessons*

Learn to do calligraphy
Go down the Colorado River
Write a movie
Direct a movie
Win an Oscar
Try cocaine
Read the great books of the Western world
Write a great book of the Western World
Get really good at golf
Get really good at tennis
Get really good at something

That was as far as I got before the drinks, the emotions, and the hour caught up with me.

I was looking for something active, challenging but easy, something hopeful, something to get me out of the damn chair. I loved the idea of winning the Iron Man Competition, or the Oscar. Learning the guitar, Italian and calligraphy were good, too. Maybe I would do them tomorrow, but I had to get through today with one small step.

And then there it was! Buy a plant and take care of it. Perfect!!

I could buy it this morning and take care of it all day. There had always been plants in my homes, which I'd enjoyed, but I had no idea as to their care and feeding. I would learn just as I would learn to nourish and care for myself. This plant and I would grow together. Of all the decisions I had ever made, this one seemed to be the wisest. My life was back on track. I hoped this plant was ready for me, because I sure as hell was ready for *it!*

At the nursery, things took an unexpected turn. I had always thought there were just two kinds of plants – big and small – but there were *hundreds*. There were plants with leaves, ferns, stalks, branches, spears and needles, plants with flowers, pods, shoots and vines, creeping, weeping, hanging and climbing plants.

Somewhere in that jungle of choices was one perfect plant just waiting for me, but which one? I didn't want to make a mistake and pick the wrong one. It's a plant; how could I pick the wrong one? Just find something that looks good and take it. No, that's too superficial, going on appearance alone. That's how I got involved with my soon-to-be ex-wife.

I was starting to feel anxious. I had managed to turn this fern into more than a plant—into a metaphor, a barometer for the journey ahead. As the plant grew, so would I. There was a hard, painful struggle waiting and all we had was me to get us through.

I realized I was in trouble and needed help, clearly psychiatric, but for the moment, botanical.

As I stood there obviously lost, a saleswoman approached to rescue me. I trusted her immediately because she was carrying a watering can. I explained I was looking for a plant but had no experience with them. She asked what it was for and I started to explain in full emotional detail. Her smile faded and she was quick to explain she meant for a home or for an office. Obviously, she wasn't into metaphors.

Regaining my composure, I explained it was for my home and she asked some plant-oriented questions about sunlight, moisture, and other things that normally apply. I had come to realize that nothing about me and this plant was normal and decided I should reconsider the Iron Man thing instead. I thanked her and on my way out through the maze of greenery, suddenly there it was: pale green, with hundreds of tiny, delicate leaves clinging desperately to fragile stems. As I leaned in for a closer look, the fronds seemed to shudder at my movement. In that moment, I knew my quest was over.

I headed toward the checkout counter and happened to

pass my saleslady. I proudly showed her my selection and once again her smile faded. I didn't know if her look of concern was for me or the plant. It was for both, given that I had chosen a maidenhair fern, the most difficult plant on earth to care for. She felt my first venture would end in failure with disappointment for me and death for the plant. She herself had tried a maidenhair fern twice and failed. She went on to explain the intricacies of the maidenhair, including the fact you don't water it, you *mist* it several times a day with Evian. And you can never touch it, leave it in direct sun or near an open window. Every warning was a new assurance that this was my soul mate because at the moment, I felt just as fragile.

I arrived home with my plant, a misting sprayer, a six-pack of Evian, two books on plant care, Myrna the saleslady's home phone number, and a bottle of a mysterious liquid I was to administer twice daily with a pipette. I could have used an eyedropper, but the pipette made it more complicated and because our survival was inexorably linked, I wanted to make it as complex a challenge as possible.

The rest of the day was spent reading my books and constantly moving the plant to find the perfect spot. Every time I found one, something in the book would give me pause: too much—or not enough—sunlight, drafts, or drying winds from the heater vents.

Staying this side of sanity, I didn't start talking to the fern...until the next day. Actually during the 4 a.m. misting. I started with just a little encouragement to go with the misting, things like, "Is this the way you like it?" which, as I write now, sounds a bit sexual, but at the time was just an icebreaker. The conversation grew with each misting and pipette treatment until, by that evening, after a couple of drinks, the fern knew the story of my life.

MR. FLORES AND ME

Two months later, the maidenhair was thriving, and, though my life was still a mess, it had started to take on a kind of grandeur and nobility: the world was changing and I was in the forefront of the upheaval ahead for marriage in general and men in particular as the Women's Movement was gaining momentum. In time, books and plays would be written, studies would be done, and the world would never be the same, but I was going through it before most people even knew it was happening. I began to see myself as a character in a Greek tragedy, suffering on a level mere mortals couldn't understand.

It was in this state I answered the door one morning and found Mr. Flores, our— now *my*—gardener. We dealt with some decisions on plants and foliage and then he stood awkwardly for a moment and said, "Excuse me señor, but. . .I don't see the señora's car here anymore and I was wondering. . ." at which point he didn't quite know what to say and frankly neither did I. How do I express to this gentle, unsophisticated man the subtleties and nuance of why he doesn't "see the *señora's* car anymore"?

With the pretension of a philosopher talking to a child, I said, "Mr. Flores, you are a gardener."

He shook his head in agreement, though not sure what that observation had do with the *señora's* car not being there, and neither did I, but I kept going:

"And people are like plants."

Agreement was edging toward confusion.

"We plant them in one place and they do well for a while, and then something changes."

He interrupted: "*Señor*, if this is about the dahlias, you're right. I'll move them—they need more sun."

"No, no, this is about the *señora's* car."

At that point he would have preferred to start transplanting the dahlias, but I persisted: "Mr. Flores, the world and people keep changing, especially in today's world, and *especially* the women... and so the *señora*—"

Here he shook his head knowingly and said, "I know, *señor*. Mrs. Flores is restless, too."

We stood nodding at one another for a moment as brothers and then he went off to move the dahlias while I stood there digesting the fact that I wasn't a character in a Greek tragedy but a new American soap opera.

LOVE & THE SEAGULL

Meanwhile, Holly was morphing into Wonder Woman: living in a funky shack in Malibu, running five miles a day, eating a macrobiotic diet, quitting cigarettes, reading Rimbaud, and learning to surf from "Keno," an 18-year-old Adonis who "just went with the waves." She was thriving while I was still fighting for survival, now smoking three packs a day and waiting for a call that she was ready to come home.

The call finally came, but it was an invitation for me to come to the beach on Saturday so we could "share our feelings." I already mentioned that it was the mid-70s and "share" had replaced the more mundane "talk about." I took a shot and told her I "knew where she was coming from," and Saturday was "cool." I had no shame.

She said, "Right on".

I threw in an "I can dig it," which I think was left over from the 50s, and hung up. It was Thursday so with just two days to get in shape, I immediately did four pushups followed by a Scotch and a cigarette.

As I drove to Malibu, I re-examined the image I planned to project because the one I had obviously wasn't working for her. To be fair to myself, her leaving had a lot to do with the emotional winds blowing through Los Angeles in 1975, as gusts from the Women's Movement played havoc with just about every marriage in town, and crosscurrents of the "anything goes" 60s were still raising dust devils.

While not holding myself blameless, the stated reason for leaving was "to find herself". I took that to mean losing me came second, but it didn't really help. I was going through a low period in my career and had just gotten custody of one of my children from my first marriage (I still can't say first marriage without a sense of failure). She had been a teenager going through a difficult time, I was an adult doing the same—all around a bad mix.

I was determined to arrive at the beach as a whole new me: upbeat, strong, a good listener with no needs of my own. I had one final cigarette—since the new me had quit—a spray of Binaca, and I was ready.

I guess I arrived early because she and Keno were out there in the surf hanging ten. I watched her glide to the beach like Annette Funicello, followed by Keno, who was more Steve McQueen than Frankie Avalon. Apparently, she hadn't seen me and headed out for another wave, looking fantastic in an orange Day-Glo wetsuit, which showed off her body. Keno was in surfer shorts featuring his body. I considered doing a thousand quick pushups but ducked behind the house and had another cigarette instead.

The next wave turned out to be the last and, as they came jubilantly out of the surf and headed toward the house, I panicked and sucked in my gut at the thought of meeting Keno. Fortunately, he turned, heading off down the beach. Suddenly, she called out, he stopped, and they ran toward each other in what looked like a Calvin Klein Infinity commercial. I watched in horror, sure they were going to have sex right there on the beach. To my relief, they just leapt in the air and high fived. If this had been a movie, I would have walked out, but it was my life and, though I didn't like my part, I had to see what happened next.

As she got to the deck, I stepped from behind the house as though I had just arrived with a clean, Keno-less slate. I managed a kind of carefree, "Hey, Babe."

She turned, we looked at each other for a long moment, and I said, indicating her wetsuit, "That's a hell of a tan."

She laughed and ran toward me. I was ready for anything from a kiss to a high five, but was happy with a long heartfelt hug and some tears.

She went to shower, which gave me a chance to have two cigarettes and toss the place for clues as to how she was spending her time and with whom. It was both humiliating and unproductive. I heard her coming and quickly got rid of the cigarette, sprayed the Binaca, and grabbed the nearest book, which happened to be Rimbaud. When she came out on the deck, there I was in the hammock with "Rim" trying to look absorbed, moved, vulnerable yet strong. Something must have worked because she joined me in the hammock and held me, once again leading to tears.

Were they tears of sadness that we were apart? Or joy that I was there? Or joy that we were apart and sadness that I was there?

Apparently, it was all of the above. She shared that she missed me but loved the freedom to be her just for her; she was lonely, but it was a good kind of lonely; she loved me, but it might not be a good kind of love.

I just kept nodding my understanding and saying, "I hear you."

It was clear the one thing of which she was absolutely sure was her ambivalence. I took that as a good sign and spent the evening being the new me, which she found very laidback and unthreatening. I acknowledged that with a kind of laidback smile and unthreatening shrug. She made a macrobiotic dinner, a once-in-a-lifetime experience, which I assured her after each new unrecognizable bite was either interesting or amazing. Fortunately, we had a lot of wine to wash it down and a lot of laughs, which always came easy for us.

All in all, it was a pretty successful outing, and when it got to be 11 p.m., it felt like time for me to leave or be invited to stay. Though I was hoping she'd ask, I wanted a cigarette so bad I would have been happy to get in the car, light up, and head to the nearest McDonald's for a quarter pounder and fries. It was an awkward moment, which I broke by saying I was leaving, giving her a gentle kiss on the forehead, and heading into the night with a walk that was mostly John Wayne with a touch of Cary Grant.

I was dying to see what effect my exit had had, but neither John nor Cary would have peeked so neither did I.

Then I heard, "Billy, stay!" It was either an invitation or, since I felt I had been such a pussy, a command to the family pet. I kept walking as if I hadn't heard. If she wanted me, let her come get me, which she did with tears, hugs, and passionate kisses.

Feeling some control for the first time, I agreed to stay but only if we went to McDonald's. It was the first honest moment of the whole day and we ended up with Big Macs, fries, and staying up half the night talking, not sharing, and smoking a pack of cigarettes.

I knew it was just a timeout from the reality, but in it we recaptured some of the good stuff that had brought us together in the first place. I lay awake after she had fallen asleep to prolong the good feelings, which were quickly fading. I have learned that reality, like the law of gravity, is going to bring you down even if you choose to ignore it. My need not to have two failed marriages, the fear of being alone and rebuilding my life from scratch, were more than I could face, so if there was a chance to prevent it, even for a moment, I would take it.

She woke at 6:30 and I was waiting with coffee and my

best impersonation of the light-hearted charmer I had been last night. Somehow, it didn't play as well in the cold, gray light of morning. Reality was back, part of it being a surfing lesson with Keno at 11:00.

I managed to take that shot to the groin without doubling over, threw in a "Cool" for good measure, and said I had a million things to do and had just been waiting for her to wake up. I was determined to get out of there with dignity. Another kiss on the forehead, followed by another "Billy, stay." Apparently, she wasn't ready to let go and said we had time to take a run on the beach.

We started off into a cold mist and I managed to keep up with her for about 10 feet, then every cigarette I ever smoked came back to haunt me. She seemed to get stronger with each stride and though she was steadily pulling away, I was determined not to let her see I couldn't keep up. After about a mile, I thought I would die, and, by the second mile, I *wanted* to die.

Suddenly, the run became a metaphor: When would I stop chasing the past? When would I stop running from change? When would I start running at my own pace in a new direction? When would I just have the heart attack I was praying for? I hoped it would be massive and kill me quickly; I didn't want to be revived getting mouth-to-mouth from Keno.

I was just about to admit to myself and to her that I couldn't take another step when, out of the mist, I heard, "Billy, come." Fortunately she added "quick," which took it out of the realm of another pet command.

When I got to her, she was doubled over at the water's edge, and for a moment I thought—O.K. I *hoped—she* had had the heart attack saving me the trouble.

Then I spotted the source of her concern: a bedraggled, dazed, and sand-covered seagull.

All animals were her natural brothers and helpless ones

her passion. During our marriage, I had rescued more of God's creatures than Noah, so this wounded gift from Heaven offered me an opportunity to not only stop running, but once again, be her hero. Suddenly, I was Dr. Dolittle as I picked up the seagull and gently examined it—for what I don't know—as she pleaded, "Billy it's so beautiful, save it. Don't let it die."

I realized I was holding not a bird but an opportunity, and never one to miss a chance to humiliate myself, said, "Are you talking about the seagull or our love?"

Oh, it gets worse.

I went on to turn the whole thing into an omen: "We didn't find this wounded creature; it found *us,* and together if we can care for it and make it strong, it can once again fly high and free just like our wounded love." I was channeling Rimbaud and snuck in some lyrics from "You'll Never Walk Alone."

I had her. We were caught up in a transcendental moment, and apparently so was the bird, which suddenly perked up and gracefully took off out to sea. As omens go, this one was a beaut. There was even a break in the mist and a ray of sunlight embraced us as we embraced each other.

Unfortunately, the bird wasn't doing as well. He suddenly stopped in mid-flight and dropped like a rock into the sea.

Another 20 feet and he'd have been lost in the fog and we might have lived happily ever after, but there he was about 30 feet out being pounded by the waves.

Once again the plaintive, "Billy, save it! Don't let our love be lost!"

If you live by the omen, you die by the omen and this one was sinking fast, so with an understated, "Never!" I stripped to my shorts and ran to the rescue.

The run slowed to a tortured walk when I hit the water, which was about 45 degrees. By the time I got to my waist, hypothermia had set in, my testicles had retreated to the top of my head and my whole body was numb, but my brain was still functioning and convinced me this wasn't worth dying for. I turned back toward the beach and the sight of her urging me on, convinced me maybe it was.

Somehow, I fought my way through the surf and actually found the gull and held it to squeals of joy from the beach. Somehow, I managed to swim back and crawl ashore still holding the bird aloft since my arm was frozen in that position. It was a magical moment as she embraced me, covered me with kisses, and was probably ready to forget Keno and come home.

The bird was not nearly as impressed as he turned and – managing to get his lower beak into my right nostril – bit down with his upper, opening a gash requiring a tetanus shot. With her tender care the seagull recovered…though our love never did.

GOODBYE MAIDEN
HAIR FERN

Over the next months, both the maidenhair and I flourished.

I became a more responsible person and father. Dana and I had worked out a pretty good life together; my new career, on my own, not only started to fall into place, but was actually taking off. The plant had doubled in size to the point that it needed a larger pot and though my books covered the procedure, I didn't want to risk upsetting things.

When I got back to the nursery, Myrna spotted us (that the plant and I had become "us" shows how important it had become). Myrna couldn't believe how beautiful and healthy it was, admitting that when I'd bought it, she hadn't given it a week. As I was waiting for the transplant, one of the sales people came up and asked if I could give some advice to a couple who were considering a maidenhair. Suddenly, I was an authority, and the strange thing is I really was. There was nothing about maidenhair ferns I didn't know and even its death had a special meaning.

After about three months of separation, I had started dating Kate, a woman who worked on one of the shows I directed. It was good to have someone find me attractive, interesting, sexy, and all the things I had lost sight of. About a month into our relationship, she invited me to spend the weekend at a condo in Santa Barbara where she was house sitting for a friend. I was ready in every way for the adventure, but actually hesitated because of the plant. I first thought of taking it along, but that would have been weird, even for me. What the hell? I would take a chance that the fern could make it through the weekend on its own. Friday night I gave it a good spraying and what I thought was an intelligent explanation for my leaving it on its own. Saturday morning dawned warm, sunny, full of promise, and a lot of ambivalence: though my heart was still with Holly, my body had been happily with Kate, and I picked her up with only a touch of anxiety, heightened by her announcement that she had scored some "primo" coke. I already felt I would be punished for leaving the maidenhair and knew I would be stopped for something like a faulty tail light, leading to search, a bust on cocaine possession and a lifetime in prison. Quickly realizing I was being ridiculous, I checked the taillights and we took off. I was almost comfortable until she produced a thermos of Bloody Marys, setting me up for a DUI as well. As we drove, I forced myself to push everything aside, except for the beautiful woman beside me, who found me attractive and had planned a romantic, if drug-filled, weekend at a beach house in Santa Barbara: still, all I could think of was what could go wrong. What did, was beyond even my concept of disaster.

Aristotle (bear with me) wrote in *The Poetics* (c. 390 B.C.) what was to become an undisputed rule for writing drama: "Probable impossibilities are preferred to improbable possibilities." In other words: it is easier to accept something that is impossible but might happen, than to accept something that might happen but is impossible. I'm not sure in which category he would put the following because it was both impossible and improbable.

By the time we turned onto the traffic packed Pacific Coast Highway, I had accepted the fact that my life was moving on as was Holly's and that while I drove with Kate's arm around me, Holly was probably in the young and powerful arms of Keno. And she was!! (Here's the Aristotle part.) In the Mercedes convertible directly in front of me was Holly. With the young and powerful arm of Keno, extended through the window.

It was improbable *and* impossible, but there they were, and for the next five bumper-to-bumper miles I couldn't get away from them. There was nowhere to turn off or back, no lane to change into, just her having an apparently joyous, disgustingly affectionate time with Keno, while Kate was trying to have the same with me as she sang along with Fleetwood Mac's, "You Make Lovin' Fun," wanting me to join in. My life was falling apart one car length ahead and she wanted me to sing!

For 30 agonizing minutes, I was like the Drama masks: on the right, Kate saw a smiling, happy guy, thrilled to be with her, while on the left was the tortured, miserable man that I was.

After the PCH I managed to salvage a pretty good weekend—maybe the cocaine helped—and managed to feel pretty good about things, until I got home and saw the maidenhair. It was in serious trouble: limp and sagging, its color faded. I couldn't believe I had so miscalculated.

I was past feeling that I, too, was doomed, but was guilty that in thinking of my own pleasure, I had let down my best friend. Then on Monday, Luberta told me that Holly had come by to pick up some things and thought my plant was dry so she watered it. A plant that was brought up on gentle misting can't just suddenly be watered. Over the next week the maidenhair went steadily downhill and no matter what I said or did I finally had to face the reality that it was over. I buried it in the yard. Just as you would the family pet.

And so, the metaphor was complete. Holly's leaving had been a shattering experience I wasn't sure I would survive.

Then, with the help of a simple plant as a symbol, I started to find my way back and reached the point where, to paraphrase Freud, "a plant is just a plant." It was only fitting Holly had ended its life because I had reached the point where I didn't need it or her anymore, and though I managed to do most of the things on my list (the Ironman and Oscar are still waiting), the maidenhair was the start of it all. A simple, almost pathetic start, but I will never forget those months when the plant and I survived, along with Dana and the ever-present Luberta Clift.

MRS. CLIFT

She was—and still is, more than 35 years later—one of the most special women in my life. Luberta Clift became our housekeeper two days before Dana moved in, and five before Holly moved out. It was hardly the job she had signed on for, telling me later that, after Holly and I had interviewed her, she had told her husband, Walter, that she just couldn't wait to go to work for us: the perfect family...which overnight consisted of a wounded 12-year-old girl and a devastated 44-year-old man. Anyone else would have made a run for it, but not Mrs. Clift.

She is the embodiment of everything a good Christian person is supposed to be, but all too seldom is. Job had it easy compared to Luberta over the first year with us, yet she neither wavered nor judged. She just kept being there, caring for us as if we were her own. She has been a part of every major event in our family, the good and the bad, for 35 years, and to Dana, Jamie, and Liza, Mrs. Clift's birthday is considered a national holiday.

None of us ever eat chicken, peas, and mashed potatoes without remembering the hundreds of Friday nights when Luberta picked the girls up at school and I came home from work to find it all warming in the oven. (Only now can I risk telling her: Luberta, your potatoes were always lumpy.) My girls and I counted on her to the point that five years after I left L.A. for New York and no longer had a house, she was still our housekeeper, the one the girls and I could depend on to be there.

The only time I had a chance to be there for her, as she had been for me, was when she was stopped by an L.A. motorcycle cop for a DUI. The strongest thing Luberta Clift ever drank was the grape juice at communion.

She had been the victim of a racist cop. Her grandchildren were in the car with her. They had been on their way home from Dodger Stadium where she was a member of the Boosters club: the only thing she loved more than the Dodgers was the baby Jesus Himself. She had swerved at the entry ramp to the freeway when she was distracted for a moment by her granddaughter squirming her way out her car seat. The siren sounded and this modern-day Nazi stopped her. The cop began humiliating her. He was also trying to provoke her enraged teenage grandson into reacting. The cop kept insulting her until she burst into tears.

When I saw her the next day, she was inconsolable, stripped of her dignity and, even more important, her faith in the goodness of all human beings. I promised she would have her day in court, and she did, with her grandson present and the toughest, most expensive lawyer in L.A. at her side. He proved this traffic stop wasn't the first racial violation by the cop who was forced to publicly apologize and was demoted to a desk job after a one-month suspension.

Her happiness over the victory was only diluted by her concern for the cop.

YOU HAD TO BE THERE

"You had to be there" usually follows the telling of some hilarious or incredible incident that the teller experienced, finishing with the expectation of either laughter or amazement, only to be met by complete silence and vacant stares. Consequently, to really appreciate that moment, "you had to be there." I hope that isn't true of what follows -- some very special moments when I happened to be "there."

DANCING WITH THE
SUPER STARS

I would give anything to be able to tap dance, but never could and never will, with the exception of one great step that I still do pretty well, along with 14 other people who will never forget it either because we learned it from Gene Kelly.

He was the guest star on a Julie Andrews special I had written and when I came in early one morning, he was already in the rehearsal hall on the phone, tap dancing as he spoke. When he saw me, he waved hello and kept on dancing, making it look so easy I knew with a little help I could do it, too.

So, when he hung up, I told him how much I would love to tap dance and he said, "Then let's tap dance!" leading me to the long wall of mirrors lining the room. "Try this," he said and did a simple step.

Suddenly feeling silly, I tried to back off, and he responded by doing the step again, and then, in the classic move of one tap dancer turning the stage over to another, stepped aside gesturing that I was "on," clapping out the rhythm until finally I did it…badly. But, after some corrections and a couple more tries, I looked pretty good.

It was at that point the waiter from the commissary wheeled in the coffee cart and, realizing there was a lesson in progress, asked if he could join in. He was a natural and a couple of minutes later, the three of us—Gene, the waiter and me—were looking like The Nicholas Brothers.

At that point, a young agent from the William Morris Agency came by to deliver some contracts and within no time he was tapping away.

We were just about ready to move on to a new step when the door opened and an NBC page stood there with 10 people he was leading on a tour. He apologized for interrupting the rehearsal and was starting to leave when Kelly invited them all to join us. So there we were: Gene Kelly, me, the waiter, the agent, the tour guide, a honeymoon couple from Vermont, a dentist from Phoenix with his wife and twin daughters, a retired mailman and his wife from Minneapolis, two sailors on leave from San Diego, and two people from China who couldn't speak English but, boy, could they dance.

But if my experience with Gene Kelly was fun, what happened with Fred Astaire was amazing.

Universal wanted him to do a television series, and, since he was a fan of *The Dick Van Dyke Show,* he wanted my partner Sam and me to write the pilot. I was more excited about meeting him than getting the job!

We met for lunch at the Universal commissary where, in addition to Astaire, we sat with Cary Grant and got to meet Ingrid Bergman and Alfred Hitchcock. When they talk about "The Golden Days Of Hollywood," that had to be one of them.

Still, the best was yet come.

We went to Fred's (he insisted we call him "Fred") bungalow to talk about the show he had in mind. He wanted to play a guy who owned a record company (which he did), and have each episode be about a song he would sing and dance to at the end. It was a really good concept and we immediately started to come up with ideas, most of which he liked. After about an hour, we were ready to start writing; all we needed was a song. He hoped we could use the one his record company called "Think Pretty," and he went over to the turntable behind his desk to play it for us.

As soon as the song started, he began to softly snap his fingers and sway in time to the music just like he did in the movies. Then he did a couple of quick steps, just like he did in the movies when he'd be waiting for Ginger Rogers, Cyd Charisse, or Audrey Hepburn to join him.

But they weren't there; Sam & I were, but we were too stunned to breathe let alone dance as Fred did a couple of slides, ended up in his desk chair, swiveled around a few times, and proceeded to dance with his umbrella...just like he did in the movies.

And we sat there, just like *we* did in the movies, watching Fred Astaire dance around, over, and with the furniture.

I guess you had to be there...and luckily, I was.

BACHELOR FATHERS

Not to be confused with *Bachelor Father,* which actually was a television show in 1967. Ours—the other fathers were my best friends, Saul Waring and Joe La Rosa—was more of a reality show that ran in a series of Hamptons summer rentals from 1977 to 1980.

Saul has been more than a brother for almost 60 years, ever since we met on my honeymoon in Bermuda. And I met Joe 15 years later when he became his business partner in Waring & LaRosa, their legendary advertising agency. In all the years we have shared vacations, houses, weddings, and funerals, we have never had an argument or failed to be there for one another, making the good times better and the bad more bearable.

Though I still lived and worked in L.A., I took that summer off and we rented a house in Westhampton. We were all divorced, all dating again, and had eight children among us, each of whom had at least eight friends. Although we often ran out of beds, we never ran out of estrogen, testosterone, teenage angst, midlife crisis, and laughter.

Food, however, was another matter as we went through enough every weekend to feed Yugoslavia, making us a major factor in the financial success of David's Cookies and Häagan Dazs ice cream.

It was a joyous time that we got to spend time with our

kids in a way we never would have, living as one big combined family with every weekend another adventure.

Our first Fourth of July at the Halsey House, however, was almost a disaster. I was finishing editing a TV movie I had directed when Saul called in panic. A friend had phoned from Westhampton to tell him that all of the markets were out of food so we'd better shop in the city.

Caught by surprise, but as the unofficial culinary leader of the group, and a director, I immediately responded: "You buy everything that grows from the ground, Joe gets everything that grows in trees, and I'll get everything else." I assigned the beverages to Herb Rowland, a friend of Saul's whom he had invited to join us.

When we got to the house on Friday night, the combined food bill was over $1,400 and the only duplication was potato chips, which I'd bought as part of "everything else," and Saul had bought because potatoes came from the ground (though, as I pointed out, not in that condition). All told, there were 30 people in residence, and by Saturday dinner we had to order pizza. Undaunted, the next day we invited 100 people to a party and fed them all.

Other weekends our Saturday night lobster dinners were a highlight with never less than 20 in attendance at a huge picnic table covered by multiple layers of aluminum foil, plastic plates and glasses, with piles of lobster, steamed clams and corn dumped on the table. At the end, we rolled up whatever was left, tilted the table into a garbage can and brought out the Häagen Dazs. I don't think we washed a dish the whole summer.

The tennis court was in action constantly, as was the sound system, alternating between Sinatra for the dads, and disco, rock, folk for the kids, and, once, for about 30 seconds, something classical (we always suspected Herb, who was an intellectual).

Saul's son Rob was a great musician, and when he came out his band came with him for our live concert parties.

As the parents, we were more conservative in our own sleeping arrangements than with the kids'. There was a new morality and we were trying to get with it, while dragging along the rules of another time. Over the summer, there were a number of mini-romances but no broken hearts. *(Well, one which is complicated, and covered in a later chapter.)*

MY SHORTEST DATE EVER

It lasted exactly one hour and eighteen minutes and though I truly can't remember her name, I will never forget something she said: The greatest line of dialogue I have ever heard.

It was on a snowy November night in 1979. I was in a period between relationships and being "fixed up" by my sister's friend, Cynthia, considered the Queen of Upper East Side Matchmaking. With her reputation at stake, she didn't take on just anybody and I'm sure my case was more a tribute to my sister than my standing on the most eligible bachelor list.

However, let's call her Delia Leopold Fournier. She and her family were right up there at the top of New York's most desirable. The "Fournier" was from her recently ended marriage to a French diplomat, millionaire, playboy, and vineyard owner. She was in New York being comforted by her parents in their Park Avenue duplex.

I was watching the first snowfall of the season from the window of my East 74th street walk-up when Cynthia called and rhapsodized for 20 minutes about Delia who had agreed to our meeting and was waiting expectantly by the phone. Because I was about to take a walk in the snow, it seemed like a kind of non-date date so I called and got a hello after the eighth ring; clearly she *wasn't* waiting by the phone.

I said, "Hi, this is Bill Persky, Cynthia's friend. Would

you like to take a walk in the snow?" The ensuing silence was so long I thought we had been disconnected.

Finally, she said, "Why?"

I could have handled a "No!" but "Why?" caught me off guard. If you don't know why you take a walk in the snow there is no way to explain it, but I tried, losing my own conviction as I went along. Even the way she listened was intimidating.

Unfortunately, somehow I made it sound like "a lark," and a half-hour later, dressed in jeans, an old parka, and Clark Chukka boots, I entered her apartment building greeted by four doormen who were about to direct me to the delivery entrance until I announced I was there for Mrs. Fournier. They obviously didn't approve but rang her apartment.

I stood waiting in the grandest lobby I have seen outside of Versailles until she appeared as a tiny speck by the elevators at the end of a long corridor, much like Omar Sharif approaching from the far distance through the heat wave distortions in *Lawrence of Arabia*. Finally she arrived, dressed for St. Moritz with a pleasant enough face that didn't know how to smile. The doormen stood ready to toss me at her whim.

Once outside, I turned left and she asked—*challenged,* actually—how I had decided which way to walk. At that point, I was ready to keep going without her, but I explained that the snow was blowing from the other direction, and also there was a nice little bar a couple of blocks down on Lexington. This seemed to satisfy her and she followed.

We said little until we got to the bar, but even in silence it was clear she was the most spoiled, arrogant, entitled person I had ever met, to the point I was actually enjoying it—sort of like visiting some kind of weird behavior museum.

After all the best schools, orthodontia, clothes, horses, and social connections, she had moved to France to study art and met Fabrian who courted her in lavish fashion, married her in someone's palace, honeymooned on his yacht, moved her into his Paris townhouse while still managing to keep up with his various business interests and two mistresses.

The evening was like listening to a Danielle Steele book on tape, one of the better ones. I had little to say since we had absolutely nothing in common and I was really caught up in her tale of the international good life.

She had begun to work and soon ran her husband's vineyard, coming to know more about wine than the Gallo Brothers and the Christian Brothers combined with Louie Martini thrown in. That gave me my first opening as I had recently tasted Schramsberg, the highly-touted champagne from California. I asked if she had tried it.

Her response was the best summing up of a character I have ever heard in just one sentence.

After her divorce, an old boy friend from L.A. flew her—by private jet, naturally—from Paris to spend New Year's with a group who would cheer her up. There was a suite waiting for her at the Bel-Air where she could sleep the jet lag away and call him when she was ready for breakfast. He had a surprise for her.

He arrived with a waiter in tow, pushing a serving cart filled with roses surrounding a huge bowl of fresh strawberries and an ice bucket in which were chilling two bottles of Schramsberg. He had just bought 200 cases and, knowing what a connoisseur she was, couldn't wait for her opinion. He opened the bottle, poured with a flourish, and waited expectantly as she sipped, considered, and sipped again.

He was on the edge of his chair as she knifed him through the heart with, "Henry, on a hot day in July…with a hamburger… *maybe*."

Take that, Noel Coward.

MIDLIFE DATING, OR HOW TO FIND THAT
CERTAIN SOMEONE. . . AGAIN

I think we can all agree that of the countless blessings and gifts God bestowed on Adam and Eve, the most magnificent and loving was that they didn't have to date.

They awakened and saw one another *"and it was good."* There were a few moments of surprise and uncertainty, but no small talk, coyness, game playing, invulnerability, thoughts they might do better, time needed to be sure, space to find themselves, or fear of commitment. She had no basic distrust and rage against men, and he had no fear or control issues with women. The world was made just for them, *"and it was good."*

That is, until they jumped headlong into Man's first contribution to Paradise: A Relationship, *"and it was bad"* because everybody they "begat" has been trying to "beget" one ever since.

For we are creatures of union and sharing, needing to love and be loved, needing not to be alone. But ours is no easy course of waking to find one another. We must seek and woo and win. As part of growing up, we experience the rite of passage: a tribal dance performed in rented dinner jackets and wrist corsages, of dry-mouthed invitations and giggling acceptances. Movies and pizza, proms and picnics, passion-steamed windshields and fumbled buttons, going steady and breaking up, loving, hurting, and seeking that one special person to whom you will "never have to say I'm sorry." The whole experience is awkward and silly, painful and joyous, and along the way you learn about yourself and how the world works.

Actually, if Adam and Eve had dated, they might have been better off. He would have learned she was impetuous, vulnerable to the suggestions of others, unable to keep a promise, and ate between meals. She would have seen that he was immature and not good under pressure. That's what dating is all about— getting to know one another, getting married, and going on to live happily ever after.

Then came the 70s, which didn't turn out all that happy and marked the end of 36 percent of the "forever afters." So many of us were out there again, with cautious ear and demanding eye, suspicions, prejudices, and a feeling of déjà vu. Yes, you have been there before, and it is still awkward, silly and painful—but, this time, seldom joyous. And even in today's texted, emailed, iMac-ed, Blackberried, Facebooked, Match.com-ed, J dated, EHarmony-ed, instagrammed twitterverse, it may be digital but it's still dysfunctional.

You resist, but, sooner or later, you relent and immediately regress to that dry-mouthed teenager you thought you had left behind. Somehow "Are you busy Saturday night?" does not fall trippingly from the tongue of a 45-year-old. You are directing the question to a lady who has come into your life in one of two ways: you have seen and selected her for yourself, or, more precariously, you have been "fixed up."

The name—"fixed up"—says it all; it implies that somehow you are broken, and because she is being fixed up with you, she must be broken, too. What a great prospect: two broken people getting together to repair one another. The only chance you have is if you happen to be broken in different places.

There is no historical record of the first blind date, but whenever it was, I bet it didn't work out. And, chances are neither will yours. Even though the "fixers" are usually good friends, it doesn't take long for the "fixee" to realize that the "fixette" is more likely to suit someone else's taste rather than yours. Sometimes the match-up can be so outlandish you wonder if your friends really know you...or even like you.

Finding someone on your own adds an element of control and adventure; you never know when or how it will happen: that chance meeting at the check-out stand of the market. Actually, it's not so chance. Anyone who has been "re-single" for long can read a shopping cart like a book.

The ten-items-or-less counter is your best bet. A larger order usually means married, or living with. Beer? There's a guy at home, unless it's light, then it could be hers. Candy? Could mean kids or a marijuana habit.

The market is also an easy place to start a conversation: "Boy, how about these prices!"

Airplanes are supposed to be great, but the closest I've been was sitting next to a guy who was on his way to Europe for a sex change. Guess I was lucky; I could have met him on the way back.

The accidental meeting is what we are all hoping for... fate stepping in to bring two people together. After a while, when you're desperate you try to give fate a hand by getting out of cabs before your destination or, in extreme cases, getting in line for a movie you didn't even want to see.

But, by whatever path you arrive, you will find yourself ringing some bell at some strange door, shining your shoes on the back of your pant leg, waiting to pick up your date. It's probably for dinner since there are very few proms in the adult world, and a movie really doesn't let you get to know one another. Somehow a waiter and a menu provide enough distraction to make the whole process bearable, and a first date is a process, like an interview to fill a position that is open in your life. It's a time to exchange emotional resumes.

There are two ways to exchange life stories: the "me you—me you" method in which you take turns, incident by incident, trauma by trauma, or the "me, me—you you" where you tell your story and she tells hers. Actually, if you choose this latter method, you should let her go first. Since you're older, your story is longer and she might never get hers in. The "me you—me you" has a number of benefits: it makes you feel as if you are actually having a conversation, and it helps to keep you alert and involved.

The "me me—you you" is like playing a part on Broadway too long; it's hard to keep it fresh. I once dozed off right in the middle of: "How I gave up my job in New York for my big break in Show Business?"

Another benefit of "me you—me you" is that you get to take turns as a listener/eater. More than once I have ended up with cold linguini during a "me me" because I got to the part about my first marriage ending just as the waiter arrived. That part has a lot of sensitivity and pain, so you don't want to break the mood to chew.

I really think first dates could be eliminated altogether if people exchanged background sheets that could be read at home beforehand. That practice would save you from those evenings that are destined to go nowhere, a realization that hits you right in the middle of your shrimp cocktail. But there's no turning back from the moment when, suddenly, the door starts to open. You consider whether to go for a boyish "Trick or treat!" or you just stand there holding in your stomach with hope in your heart that this will be it. If not forever, then at least for a while. They say "It only takes one," but I've gone through some bizarre twists and turns on the road to finding *her*. Most blend into a collage of hopeful but disappointing dinners, a lot of two or three date "This could be its" and some that, for me, went on long past "this isn't it, but I'm staying anyway.

10 MILES TO
TOCCOPOLA

When I saw the roadside sign I was in Mississippi, driving a Ryder truck with a steering wheel the size of a manhole cover, a pack of Kents rolled up in my T-shirt sleeve, drinking a Dixie beer with Cassie beside me smoking a joint, and thinking to myself, "What the hell am I doing in Mississippi, 10 miles from Toccopola, driving a Ryder truck, with a steering wheel the size of a manhole cover. . .etc.?"

Once again I was going the extra mile in my never-ending pursuit of love. The day before I had been wearing an Armani suit, driving a Mercedes convertible and the sign said, "Welcome to Universal Studios" where I was shooting a television pilot. That's a long way—emotionally, intellectually, socially, and sanely— from Toccopola. It started with her name: Cassis Cloud, which sounded like an exotic drink with a parasol. She was captivating and delightful, but the relationship was doomed from the start. She was also southern and Catholic, so between the charm and guilt – hers and mine – we never stood a chance. (Just as a point of information: there is a big difference between Jewish and Catholic guilt. With Jewish guilt you spend your life doing things for the person you hurt to make up for it. With Catholic guilt you do even worse things to the person because they made you feel guilty.) It's a deadly combination but what romantic fool could resist? Especially with a name like Cassis Cloud ? Certainly not this one, so for five years I…rather than the humiliating details, I think the song I wrote tells the story.

10 MILES TO TOCCOPOLA

Ten miles to Toccopola
That's what the signpost read
That means that she and heartache
were just 10 miles ahead.

If you never loved a Southern girl
Then you won't understand
How they can make most any man
A puppet in their hand.

They all have a sad sad story
Told in a lilting drawl
How they've been hurt and cheated
And you want to fix it all.

They tell it with a wistful look
A flutter of the eyes
A wind chime laugh and honey voice
that melts the toughest guys.

Five miles to Toccopola
Exit 20 N
And though I know it's going to hurt
I'm chasing it again.

We had three months of wonder
So perfect at the start

MY LIFE IS A SITUATION COMEDY

A year of breakup/make-up
Until it fell apart.

I got calls from Dallas
Miami and L.A.
"Darlin', I need you"
And I was on my way.

Entering Toccopola
Time to play the game
Falling tears and promises
It's always just the same.

I was in New York City
The phone woke me at two
The machine picked up and at the beep
"If you're there, my precious, I need to hear your voice."

And one more time I picked it up
As if I had a choice.

Now I'm at the exit ramp
And then the cloverleaf
A left will lead me safely back home
A right leads me to grief.

Leaving Toccopola for the final time
And though my heart is heavy
I know it's best that I'm
Leaving Toccopola.

One funny memory of those journeys was the first time I was passing through Ocean Springs, Mississippi and saw a road sign that read: MISS OCEAN SPRINGS JUNIOR COLLEGE and thinking, "I knew beauty contests were big in the South, but I didn't expect they would name a college after one."

WORKING IT OUT

After Cassie, everyone was looking to fix me up, but I just wanted to get back to my study of Calligraphy and classical guitar, two things I turn to at the end of relationships, figuring I will eventually end up as a Trappist monk, recopying the book of Kels – maybe as a musical.

Then along came Nancy and the book of Kels was once again put on hold. Nancy had looks, charm, a career and a great life of her own. She also had a young child and after raising three of my own, I was determined not to do it again. But as it turned out, my determination was no match for my attraction and we started "working it out" which was the titte of the TV series the relationship inspired. It starred Jane Curtin, Steven Collins and 8 year old Kindra Kaster, who I had chosen rather than 8 year old Christina Ricci, whom I wisely decided didn't have star quality. (In defense of my eye for talent, two years later I cast Claire Danes as Dudley Moore's daughter in a pilot, and CBS decided she didn't have star quality.)

Each week, "Working It Out" followed the gradual, tentative development of the relationship, from the first meeting in a cooking class, through the first date, the first kiss, the first doubts, the first…everything. The reviews were fantastic: 27 raves from all around the country, the only ones I ever saved. The people who saw it loved it but at 8 o'clock Saturday night most of the people it was about weren't home to watch a relationship—they were out trying to find one.

I asked the NBC head of programming, Warren Littlefield, to move it and since the show was getting such great reaction he said he'd consider it. After 13 weeks, without a day or a minute off as head writer, producer and director, I was exhausted. I decided if I was going to die doing this show, I wanted to at least have a chance to be a hit and told Warren if we didn't get a better time slot, I just couldn't keep doing it.

Due for a break, I went to Canyon Ranch in Tucson to recuperate. Every part of me was in need of repair: I even had my first, and last, facial and a pedicure. Three days later, when Warren called with his decision, my feet were soaking in hot wax, my hands were vibrating in pink herbal mud-filled mitts and I had cucumber slices on my eyes. In a deeply serious voice he said they wouldn't change the time slot and I, in an equally serious voice, sounding bizarre coming from a man with cucumbers on his eyes, told him I wouldn't do it anymore.

Though the show and the relationship are long gone, happily the child, Danielle – now 35 and a fabulous young woman – remains a much-loved member of our family.

MY ALBINO WARD

I met Danielle when I picked Nancy up for our first date and was smitten yet again: she was a nine year old version of her mother. She had an angelic face, framed by a cascade of golden curls and she was wearing a white applique Princess nightgown. When the two of them stood together you expected Richard Avedon to show up and photograph them for vogue. Danielle's first impression of me, I learned later, was less spectacular. She told Nancy: "He looks very old."

The relationship with Nancy started out great – full of fun, romance and promise, with my rule about no more kids, no match for the irresistible Danielle. Her view of me changed when she came to a taping of "Kate & Allie," which was exciting, especially when she developed a crush on Freddie Koehler, who played Allie's son, and whom I "encouraged" to be charming. Danielle and I took a leap forward when I was invited by Susan St. James to be the auctioneer at a fundraiser for the Special Olympics at a Connecticut ski resort, which was the first time the three of us went away together; they shared a room. We skied, rooted for the Special Olympics kids in their competitions, and then went to the dinner where I was a huge hit. Danielle was impressed, but the most meaningful moment for her was that it was the first time she had ever seen her mother dance with a man, and she started to view me as a great guy: something new in her experience of men. Her father wasn't a part of her life any longer and when he had been, was not a very happy one and, although her mother had dated, none of the men had made much of a connection with Danielle. Things were looking good.

Without getting into a lot of psychological conjecture, it was clear from the start that for Nancy, Danielle came first, last and always, with very little room for anyone else. They were a team and the best you could become was a fan. Danielle was going to the best schools and, with Nancy's urging and support, was an honor student, a great athlete, and already creating an impressive résumé for what Nancy wanted to be a golden future. She was a fantastic mother: caring, loving, supportive and committed. It was a full time job leaving little room for me on any deep level. But, instead of taking that as a problem I made it a challenge, convinced that in time, my importance to them both would prevail. The only one who was thriving was Danielle, who had found a father figure at last. She loved me, as I did her, and she trusted me in all things. I was friend, advocate, confidante and teacher in all guy things. I admit the following with a mixture of pride and embarrassment: I stayed longer than I should have, mainly because I didn't want Danielle to feel that in the end, you really couldn't trust a man. As noble as that may seem, it was more a sign of my "save the woman" issue than my virtue and hardly made me a candidate for the cover of Mental Health Magazine. Whatever the cause, the result was worthwhile as Danielle continued to rely on me after the relationship ended and she became part of my family, as Dana, Jamie and Liza considered her their little sister.

When she graduated Wellesley summa cum laude and captain of the lacrosse team, her mother was ready for her to conquer Wall Street, but by then Danielle had had enough of achievement and took off for Alta, Utah, and the life of a ski bum. Her mother was crushed that after all the planning, devotion and sacrifice, Danielle would end up coming down a mountain rather than scaling it. I had always told Nancy that she was creating a résumé Danielle wasn't going to want to live.

The next couple of years were full of rebellion for Danielle and angst for Nancy, while I became the confidante for both sides, as her mother finally accepted me as a full-fledged member of the team. By then I was married to Joanna who had inherited the concern for three stepdaughters along with the concern for one young woman for whom there was no official designation: not a daughter (step or otherwise), more than a friend, the one with the golden mane among the brunettes in a family photo, the one whom Joanna dubbed, "Our Albino Ward."

Just a word here about my wife, Joanna, or actually, a sly compliment to myself: after all the mistakes and false starts I finally got it right. How many women would lovingly accept and embrace the daughter of the husband's ex girlfriend? She was there, along with Nancy, supportive through a couple of failed relationships, understanding through her struggle to find a purpose and direction for her life and proud, alongside Nancy as Danielle won top honors on her graduation from the French Culinary Institute. Graduation was the start of her career as a chef. Whatever my reasons, neurotic or not, Danielle is a joyous part of my life and I look forward to the day, when the right guy comes along, and I walk her down the aisle.

JOANNA

If I had made a wish list of everything I could think or dream or fantasize of in a woman, I would have short-changed myself because, until I met Joanna, I didn't even know what was possible. Unfortunately when I first met her 30 years ago, boy did I miss it!

Joanna is the woman mentioned earlier who claims to this day, following 16 years of marriage, that I left her with a broken heart on the doorstep with her bags packed after a one-week romance in 1977 during the summer of "The Bachelor Fathers." (See the above chapter.) Obviously every story has two sides, and mine always provokes sharp pokes in the ribs: She still carries a grudge. What follows is my version and when Joanna writes a book, she can tell hers.

During that summer of 1977, I, along with most single men my age (35-45), was pursuing all the societal, social and sexual freedoms that we weren't ready for in the 60's because of our more traditional upbringing. During the 40's and 50's we all had wallets with the embossed circular badge of manhood: the condom we carried through high school and never got to use. Then most of us were divorced with kids, alimony and more than enough responsibilities, so we weren't looking for a commitment beyond, "would you like another drink?" If the scenario sounds selfish, it was, but most young women at that point were busy pursuing their new career possibilities and were just as willing to be "unencumbered."

The Bachelor Fathers, Joe and Saul and me, went out with a number of terrific women that summer, most of whom remain friends to this day, with Joe and Liane happily together 35 years later. Saul was a serial dater and could be in the *Guinness Book of Records* for most dates in a lifetime, until he finally met and married Willa. (The only way to meet a woman in New York he hadn't dated was to wait outside of immigration.) The first time I saw Joanna, she was having dinner with Saul and I fell immediately in love, or whatever it was I was falling into at that time. She literally took my breath away, as she still does.

She was Saul's date on a few weekends at the house, and I realized that her looks were the least of how special she was. She was smart, funny, warm and all around wonderful: Dana, Jamie and Liza met her only once and liked her better than anyone I dated before or after. (At this point Joanna would deliver the first poke in the ribs).

By the end of August it was clear the feelings were mutual and when I drove Joanna back to the city one Sunday, we felt we should do something about what was going on. Of course I asked Saul if it would be O.K. (another jab) and it was fine because he had expected my request. So the week before I went back to work in L.A., after an incredible few days together, she "assumed" (several hard pokes) or "understood" she was going back with me. (Joanna's note on reading this: "You asked me VERY SPECIFICALLY to move to L.A. You said 'I'm going back to L.A. and you'll come out and live with me.' And I said 'O.K.' and went and packed my suitcase and sat on the stoop and waited".)

In my defense I was unaware of her expectations (poke). Add insensitive, (two pokes) stupid, thoughtless, callous, boorish and anything you wish to add (from Joanna: "Try *asshole*") but I knew that once back in L.A., I was faced with too many unresolved problems – including children and career – to make such a serious commitment. (Major jab).

When I moved to New York in the 80's to do *Kate & Allie*, I would run into Joanna on occasion, but had no idea of my failure as a human being because she was always just…Joanna: warm and wonderful. In 1994, when my relationship with Nancy, Danielle's mother, ended, so did at last did my pattern of looking for a woman to validate who I was. I nominated myself as a decent person, seconded it, and it was passed unanimously. Not looking to get involved in anything serious and always enjoying Joanna's company, I called to ask her if she was free to have dinner. I reached her answering machine and left the following message: "Hi, it's Bill Persky, and if you're not involved with anyone, neither am I and would you like to have dinner?"

I didn't hear back for three weeks. She was in Europe on business for the first two and then one week because she hated me.

Fortunately her niece, Amanda, was staying at her loft in Soho while she was away and had heard the message, which Joanna erased the second she recognized my very distinguishable voice. When Joanna arrived at her office the next day, Amanda and several of the other women in the office asked, "Are you going to go out with the guy with the voice?" Amanda thought I sounded very interesting. Joanna assured Amanda and everyone else that the man who was attached to that voice was of no interest to her. Over the next week, with encouragement from Amanda and some second thoughts of her own, she called and invited me to a dinner party at her apartment. I went. And we have been together ever since.

We never discussed marriage. Nor did I ever officially propose: It was just the logical step to make perfect even better.

I never actually said: "Will you marry me?" but came up instead with a truly unromantic statement of fact. My part is memorable for its absurdity, her acceptance because it is so perfectly Joanna. We were walking down Fifth Avenue after a lovely dinner on a perfect spring evening. While waiting for a light, I took her in my arms, looked into her eyes and said: "You know I love you, but I want to be clear about what I can handle and what I can't. I have raised my three kids, taken care of my parents, and really can't deal with a lot of complications."

She considered for a moment and said, "I have no children. My mother, father and brother are dead. Do you want me to kill my sister?"

We were married four months later and I've had the happiest 16 years of my life. At this point she would deliver a series of pokes, insisting that it could have been 35 years, but I don't think so. Looking back at the wins and losses, the good and the bad in my life, I think I am right where I should be and so is just about everyone. I wrote a song called, "I wouldn't be where I am, if I wasn't where I was," and I really believe that lyric. Joanna and I got together when we were supposed to. Neither of us was the person in 1977 that we became in the intervening years and I wouldn't give up any of the experiences I've had along the way. I don't think Joanna would either.

She, her sister Judy Lotas, friends Karen McIver and Sally Minard founded an advertising agency, Lotas Minard Patton McIver that grew to be the largest agency in the world owned and run by women, employing over 100 people with 3 floors in the Carnegie Hall Tower. They were hot stuff with international clients, lots of awards, money, good times and incredible experiences, none of which would have happened if she had moved to L.A. She also had a number of relationships that were important to who she is now, although she didn't need any improvement.

LOTTIE

What is it like to wake up four days shy of your 94th birthday to yet another moving day? Only Lottie Persky knew as she opened her eyes to the blurred shapes that were all her "legally blind" vision let in. I'm sure she thought her final morning in Florida would be the end for her rather than yet another beginning. She was leaving everything she knew for a world my sister Bunny and I were creating for her.

In New York City, Bunny and I woke to our own experiences of apprehension and anxiety, which may mean the same thing, but on this day there was enough of both to go around.

Maybe we should have left things as they were. What was it that made this seem like it was the thing to do? The money? For sure, the idea of getting help from Medicaid was a factor. My mother's well being? Our well being? I wonder if everything just snowballed and we just got too caught up.

She was there in Florida, living a life that had a routine and although she was dependent on others, the familiarity gave her a kind of independence she wouldn't have up north.

There was no answer that held up from one attack of angst to the next, but by and large, it seemed the thing to do for reasons ranging from humanitarian and financial to self-serving and neurotic.

The biggest thing to establish was that just because she

would be here didn't mean we'd have to be involved constantly. When she was in Florida, most of her time was spent alone and resting so that anything more here of family or social life would be a plus. A person who, for many years, had been a concept was about to become a very large reality.

Bunny and I arrived at LaGuardia an hour early, not wanting to be late for something neither of us wanted to happen at all. We each drank a cup of coffee and ate some really great yogurt pretzels (from the Nuttery in the Delta terminal; I've had them since under less stressful circumstances and they are the best). We ate with the gusto of a last meal. Fortunately, we shared our feelings as well as the pretzels and were totally honest about our ambivalence. Through our whole conversation we never took our eyes off the window waiting for the plane to come into view.

I think it was some kind of test to see what spontaneous reaction its appearance would set off. Or, maybe it was like keeping your eyes open during the scary part of a movie to see if you could handle it. If there had been musical scoring, mine would have been the theme from *2001: A Space Odyssey.*

As we gazed out the window at the tarmac, the nose of the plane edged its way into view in an almost surrealistic glide. It was just there and then stopped, my heart along with it. Bunny decided the plane stopped because my mother had an attack of some kind. The thought that a plane had a purpose or problem unrelated to our mother was never a consideration.

In those brief few moments, I felt I was still between two worlds: the one without my mother as a full time responsibility and the new one with all its restrictions. There were only moments left before the exchange would take place.

Finally the plane made a turn to the gate. The nose was enormous and seemed aimed directly at Bunny and me. What a fitting end to have it crash through the terminal and kill us. I think at that moment Bunny might have preferred that scenario.

The deplaning process was endless, like a clown car at the circus, the passengers coming in numbers beyond the capacity any plane could hold. If you didn't know the flight was from Ft. Lauderdale you might have thought it was from Lourdes: the passengers didn't have carry on, they *were* carry on, and some close to carrion as an unending stream of broken bodies and spirits in wheelchair after wheelchair rolled past.

The flight was unusually crowded because parents were also making the northward trek for Passover with their children, most of whom were on social security themselves. I'm sure as much as we considered ourselves separate and apart, Bunny and I blended right into the pack. Nothing reduces people of all strata to a common denominator like the presence of their parents.

As the stream of mothers, fathers and in rare cases, mothers and fathers, slowed to a trickle, we were now into cases with IVs and oxygen, yet there was still no Lottie. All kinds of fears and fantasies took over. She had missed the plane, died, panicked and was under restraints. I moved down the jetway to the plane itself and saw four wheelchairs circling.

It calmed me because I was sure one of them was for her. I also knew she was in good hands given that Barbara, her long time housekeeper and companion, had made the trip with her and would stay until Lottie had settled in. The Gulf War didn't have as much planning, support staff, and equipment as my mother's invasion of New York.

Her apartment, which Bunny and I had subleased and furnished, was a combination of *House Beautiful* and *The AMA Suppliers Guide*. I think Bunny took a bold step into a new dimension with the creation of a Laura Ashley hospital bed complete with dust ruffle (we have a patent pending on that one). They say everything has a reason in one's life and presents an opportunity for growth, so this could be the beginning of a new design line for senior citizens who take care of senior citizens. I think it's the hot demographic group of the future.

The whole process is kind of make-it-up-as-you-go-along since even the self-help section at Barnes & Noble doesn't have anything to cover it. I did notice *How to Take Care of an Older Parent and Still Have a Life of Your Own* and will pick it up as soon as I find time from taking care of my older parent to have a life of my own.

The foregoing was written on April 10, 1995, as the first entry of what was to be a record of my mother's adjustment, and ours, to this very dynamic change in all of our lives.

From the minute she arrived, the adjustments were so overwhelming I never had time to follow through. Either my sister or I saw her every day as the pressure of her medical and general care became a constant in our lives. Forms and files fill your life; money, even with government programs for which you should qualify, goes out with frightening regularity. The bureaucracy of age is humiliating, debilitating, and never-ending. Guilt is a constant no matter how open-hearted you try to remain. And there was a tightness in my stomach I didn't realize was there until she passed away and gradually, along with the sadness, the pressure of her day-to-day care was put to rest along with her.

Looking back, there were as many good times as bad, laughter as well as tears, and we all learned a lot about Lottie and even more about ourselves. In the midst of it all, I swore I would not let my old age become anyone's problem but my own, putting away the money and making the plans to save my children from the "burden."

But now I'm not sure they should be completely removed from that part of my life. The weight of the responsibility is counterbalanced by an abundance of pleasure and satisfaction. It's not about becoming your parent's parent; that starts earlier, when you're old enough to run your own life and when they are less able to run theirs.

This experience was deeper, gentler, and more loving. It was the pleasure one can derive from really enjoying ice cream on a warm summer evening, along with the recollection of perfect ice cream cones and picnics.

Lottie died on Mother's Day, 1997. She'd had a great day, which included a Big Mac, more talked about than eaten. How appropriate: a party with her family. When the dishes were done, she said good night. And in her sly, quiet way, she managed to claim Mother's day as her very own: all these years it was up for grabs, being about mothers in general, but now, for us, it's the day the world lost Lottie.

I honestly believe she would still be alive today, at 107, if it weren't for Joanna. Lottie wasn't going to leave until she was sure I was in good hands, with someone she could count on to see I was O.K. I think one of the happiest moments of Lottie's life was our wedding day when Joanna and I twirled her around the dance floor in her wheel chair and she christened Joanna her "daughter-in-love."

SOME CALL THE
WIND MARIAH

Although Joanna remains "more than I could have hoped for," there are certain details of everyday living that are beyond her. Or, perhaps it is *she* who is beyond *them:* time, phone numbers, dates, names, directions, locations…all considered meaningless details. I'd trust her with my life, but not to meet me on the northwest corner of 57th and Lexington. (Actually, that's a bad example because there's a great shoe store on that corner that she would hardly consider a meaningless detail.) I know that if she thought any of it really mattered, she would learn it all in a second, but she views them as "guy things"; which just might explain what happened to Amelia Earhart.

Through it all she has said and done countless things that surprise, delight and amaze me. Her foray into the world of windsurfing somehow captured it all: the humor, the spirit, the essence that is Joanna.

We were on vacation in St. Barts and more for me than for herself, she decided to take a windsurfing lesson. I knew it wouldn't be easy given that her relationship with the wind is stormy, even on the calmest of days. This otherwise bright woman is totally incapable of understanding its direction even with a flag flapping in her face, as her hat is blown from her head, while watering the lawn and she is the only thing getting wet. I think it's a form of dyslexia.

To explain that the wind is coming from the east just confuses the issue because east is always left of the direction she is facing rather than a fixed and universally-accepted position on the planet. I have surrounded her with memory crutches such as: "Where does the sun rise?" to which she responds: "In the living room." It's hard to argue her logic because the living rooms of both our homes happen to face east.

I had learned through two failed marriages that a husband cannot teach a wife anything. Although "obey" has only recently become politically incorrect in the vows, "will not take instruction" has been there since Adam and Eve.

With that in mind, I arranged for Vincent, the best teacher on the island, to instruct her. Though his heavy French accent might make it more difficult to understand his explanations of the wind's vagaries, it would allow me to interpret and therefore editorialize: "I promise to manipulate (for the bride), control (for the groom) whenever possible" is an unstated but understood part of the vows for both parties.

As we drove to the lesson, I stopped on a hill overlooking the cove where the windsurfers were already flying back and forth in a nice steady 20-knot breeze clearly coming from the east. As big fleecy clouds flew toward us and flags on the beach fluttered briskly in the same direction, Joanna offered, without a living room in sight, "The wind is coming from there."

I took it as a sign that everything was going to work out, and I'm sure if we had taken the lesson in the car on that hill, it would have. Unfortunately, on the beach it wasn't as easy.

Just standing on a windsurf board and maintaining balance is challenge enough without the cumbersome sail— weighing about 75 pounds—which starts in the water and has to be pulled upright until the wind hits, blowing it—and probably you—into the water.

Knowing even the most enthusiastic pupil would quickly give up, the school employs a teaching device that removes the need for balance and water. It's a four-foot section of a board fixed to a swivel base on the beach fitted with a small sail allowing you to deal with the basics without the obstacles. Before the lesson, to help things along, I explained to Vincent the nature of Joanna's wind deficiencies in such detail that she went back to the car and refused to get out unless I agreed to stay at least 100 yards away.

We settled at 50 and I took a position downwind so their conversation would blow toward me and I could make notes on what I wanted to correct when I had her to myself.

Not surprisingly, they quickly hit an impasse. As she got on the learning board and faced Vincent, he pointed out that the wind, as it should, was blowing from behind her. She turned to look. Feeling it on her face immediately challenged his sense of direction. Even with fluent English, he would have been no match for her inability to grasp that the wind was the constant here, coming from the direction of its choice whether you liked it or not, and you had to just accept it and go along. Because Vincent was unwavering in his conviction and Joanna didn't want to hurt his feelings, she made believe she agreed with him. I made a note to double his tip and waited for the next confrontation.

It came immediately as he started to explain how the sail is used to steer by tilting it forward to "come off of the wind" (turn away from it), and tilt back to "come up into the wind" (turn toward it). Of course, she wanted an explanation of why that was necessary. After trying in broken English to no avail, and resorting to French and finally tears, Vincent got her to accept the concept on blind faith.

Though I couldn't see her face, I knew that her eyes had glazed over, and though she seemed to be paying attention, he had lost her. The rest of the lesson consisted of a lot of pointing by him to where the wind was coming from, and her back to the wind, throwing sand in the air to see it blow away. Throwing handful after handful, she was on the verge of understanding when the gods played one of their cruel tricks; the wind shifted and the next handful came back in her face. She had just begun to trust the wind. And it turned on her.

On that sorry note, her hour was up and I went to give her a hug for a valiant effort, as well as a towel to wipe the sand from her eyes. I complimented her on a great try and assumed her interest was gone with the wind. To my surprise, and Vincent's chagrin, she wanted another hour.

Though the wind still confused her, it was now beginning to piss her off, a mistake when dealing with Joanna. For the next hour, she did battle with the combined forces of sail, board, wind, and water. She lost, but only the battle; the war was to continue after lunch.

Mistake! But I also knew the worst thing I could do was offer any suggestion, observation, comment, or criticism. Unfortunately, I didn't realize the danger extended to answering a question.

As we looked at surfers going from the beach to the reef at the far end of the lagoon, there were others coming in the opposite direction from the reef to the beach. The question, "If the wind is coming from there (indicating the inlet to our right), and it's blowing those guys to the reef, where is the wind coming from that is blowing these guys in the opposite direction at the same time?"

Unfortunately, the answer is that the wind from the same direction is blowing them both in opposite directions. It took Archimedes and Pythagoras years to figure that out, so Joanna was not about to accept it on my say so.

After lunch Joanna was ready to start again, but

fortunately, Vincent was already booked. Unfortunately, she decided to continue on her own, which meant I would be forced to get involved: not by her need, but my own to never leave well enough alone. I was subtle in my approach, pacing the shore like a first-time father in the waiting room expecting the doctor to come begging for his help.

The call never came. This contretemps was between her and the wind, and both were relentless.

Watching a hundred falls and a hundred and one rises, I fell in love with her all over again. There is just something about the way she makes even her awkwardness have style and grace. Though I have come to expect it, I am still surprised by how consistently she is who she is, taking things—but not herself— seriously. She maintains no running judgment of success or failure, always at the core maintaining a sense of humor, and herself.

Finally, at about 4 o'clock, the wind died down or just gave up for the day, having met its match. What started out as a hundred-to-one shot was beginning to look like even money. I thought it best not to offer any suggestions based on what I had observed, deciding to wait until she asked.

After a full five minutes, I felt I had waited long enough and casually mentioned I had noticed a couple of things that might help. She casually suggested I keep them to myself. It had been a great day with no serious injuries or marital confrontations and just as we were about to leave, with our marriage and bodies intact, the wind came up again and she decided on going one more round.

She headed back to her board ready to take the challenge. I suggested tomorrow was another day and was informed there was no tomorrow for her and windsurfing. There was only today and if the wind wasn't giving up, neither was she.

I drove to a spot where I could watch her, unobserved, and tried not to have any thoughts that might reach her. For about an hour she persisted and finally, as the sun was about to set, she actually sailed the board for about 40 feet until she fell. Then she climbed back up and did it again. To this day, I have no idea if she knows how she did it, but she did it, like everything, in her own way, in her own time.

When I got back to the beach, she was waiting in the parking lot looking very much like Poseidon's daughter, and I could almost hear the Beach Boys playing "Surfer Girl" in the background. When I asked how it went, she tossed her beach bag into the car, looked out to sea and replied, "The Wind calls me Mariah"

JUMPING THE SHARK

That's the term used to indicate that a series has seen its best days and is on its way out. It comes from an episode of *Happy Days*, considered the beginning of the end, when The Fonz went water skiing and actually jumped over a shark. The perception is that you have run out of fresh ideas and are reaching in desperation to keep the show going.

Though I haven't yet jumped and look forward to many more great episodes, with children grown, pages more remembered than being written, the quest for love fulfilled and enjoyed rather than sought after and fraught over, and a body that is pushing the limits of its warranty, my episodes seem to be dealing more with reality than adventure, with lessons learned and truths that you can deny but not avoid.

AN EXCITING NEW
CAREER AFTER 70

Just when you thought you were ready to retire, you're actually entering a new line of work: The Maintenance Business—A non-profit group of individual contractors whose primary function is staying alive as pain-free, stress-free, guilt and depression-free as possible. It's tough work and the only reward is, if you do it right, and you're lucky, you get to do it again tomorrow.

So far, there is no instruction manual or "How To" book, but after my own on-the-job training, I offer here a couple of insights.

The average Maintenance man is on at least two of the following prescription drugs: a statin for cholesterol, something for arthritis, high or low blood pressure, back, eyes, digestion, and prostate or sleep problems.

Then there are the commercials for diseases you're sure you have, and with every new symptom, you do as told and "ask your doctor." It adds up to about 10 pills a day, plus vitamins, Metamucil, allergy and digestive aids.

Beside the cost, a major concern is scheduling since most should be taken with meals. The good news is they replace dessert, which is great for cholesterol and diabetes. The rest are spread throughout the day and are taken with a full glass of water making 8 p.m. the end of the safety zone for those with prostate issues. If you need something to sleep taken at bedtime, you have created the perfect storm.

If you're on the job long enough, you'll be faced with the breakdown of some equipment and the choice to fix, replace, or live with it. The decision rests on the importance of the part and how long you hope to stay in the business. As a result, you will get involved with a series of doctors since there is now one specializing in each of your body's 289 parts. The one stop GP of your youth is more of a travel agent than a healer sending you on a never-ending journey to "the right guy for this."

Doctor visits are a big part of your new career and learning some simple rules will help mentally, if not physically:

Take your time filling out the forms. Among the simple pleasures of senior life is checking off "no" in succession in the "have you had any of the following" section of the questionnaire you get on the first appointment with a new doctor. It's like trying to make all the synchronized traffic lights going up Third Avenue in Manhattan without having to stop. You'll soon realize they don't read those forms; they're just there to keep you busy because the doctors are never on time and want to keep you occupied so you won't notice. Psychiatrists don't have those questionnaires because they charge by the hour, so they are always on time, and they *know* you're crazy or you wouldn't be there. Don't get upset until you have waited at least an hour after your scheduled appointment time.

Get *them* to handle the insurance and try to get samples of any and all prescription drugs; even if you're not taking them now, you probably will and/or know someone who is.

Exercise is important for the body but don't waste time remembering how good you used to be (this also pertains to sex).

Two good friends are also needed for your maintenance since three is the perfect number to recall the dates, places, and names that don't really matter but cause untold concern just because you can't remember them. Memory will start to go, especially when you wake at 3 a.m. desperately needing to remember the name of a bit player in a movie you didn't even like. Since it's too late to call the other two-thirds of your recall team, the alphabet is a handy tool. If you run through it a couple of times and still haven't found the name, you'll probably fall back to sleep in the process. When you find you can't remember the alphabet, it's time to see "the right guy for that."

Naturally, your family and possessions have all aged right along with you and constantly need repairs and extra care, as does the family pet. You've had him since he was a pup or a kitten so, in animal years, he's older than you. Do whatever it takes to keep him going, because given the opportunity, he would do the same for you.

Most important: as you enter this next phase of your life, be sure to maintain a sense of humor.

ALTERNATIVE MEDICINE
RUN AMOK

With one click of the mouse, I went from being a respected 79-year-old tenant of my co-op to receiving disapproving looks in the elevator and hearing stifled laughter as I passed. The cause? A deluge of porn and sex toy catalogues started to arrive in my mail from Foxy.com.

It started innocently with the onset of neuropathy, a mild but annoying numbness caused by lack of stimulation to the nerves—in my case, those of the right foot. There is little research and no known cure, which is why I turned to my personal miracle man, Dr. Howard Abeloff, a physiatrist (as little known a word as neuropathy) but a lifesaver for everything from bad backs and insomnia to hair loss.

Abeloff came into my life after I was scheduled for major back surgery. He was recommended by a trainer at my gym whom he had healed after an accident that had left her unable to walk. As I watched her leaping joyously in her aerobics class, I thought of Estelle Reiner's famous line in *When Harry Met Sally* and decided, "I'll have what she's having."

My first appointment with Abeloff almost ended when I opened the door to his office which was reminiscent of the bar scene in *Star Wars*, filled with a bizarre assortment of patients reading old magazines, including an ancient copy of *Look* with Grace Kelly on the cover. As I turned to leave, his associate, an

Indian woman in a sari, said, "I know it looks weird, but he will help you." And he did.

In the past three years, he has saved me, and friends, from countless operations and untold pain through methods you are more likely to find in books on witchcraft than modern medicine.

His cure for the neuropathy expanded even his boundaries when he prescribed a Trojan mini-vibrator to be inserted in…I held my breath for what might come next, and exhaled with relief when he said my sock, a location I'm sure the Trojan company had never considered. Abeloff had discovered that vibrating recharged the nerves and, in time, corrected the condition.

I nervously entered Duane Reade looking for a male cashier and felt reduced to my teenage self when I had bought my first condom, the one guys carried in wallets for so long it created an embossed circle in the leather. Walter, without a trace of judgment, directed me to the personal hygiene section where I found the mini in a finger-shaped device along with a selection of circles, rings, loops, and bullets. On checking out, I told Wilma, the only cashier available, that my doctor had prescribed it for my neuropathy, which judging from her expression, she thought was a venereal disease or a part of the male anatomy that shows up after 70.

I immediately slipped the mini into my sock and it actually helped as I chalked up another miracle to Abeloff. The only problem was that the batteries lasted just 50 minutes, probably ample time for its primary purpose but not for mine, which required continuous vibration. Obviously, I needed a rechargeable version, and turned to Google, which opened a new world of vibratory possibilities in amazing shapes, sizes, colors, materials, promises, and testimonials available from hundreds of colorful sites: pocket-rocket, smittenkitten, discreet-romance, lovehoney, Igor the Octopuss (the Godzilla of vibrators), Fantasiaparty,

Dearlady, Adam&Eve, Too-Timid, Goodvibes, Rapidrabbit, and Dr. Approved where I was relieved not to find any reference to Abeloff.

An exhaustive search from site to site left me with a feeling of sadness for all the lonely and unfulfilled people there are out there, but a new respect for the creativity and depravity of the human mind. After trying to imagine "where and how" and "what went into what," I was about to give up when I found it: The Lelo Egg, a harmless looking but effective item "available in a soft-to-the-touch finish with a floral design in pink, black, or white, with discreet carrying case and AC/DC re-charger. Due to the intimate nature of the product, there is a no return policy," this last of which I found reassuring.

I searched for a phone number because the last thing I wanted was to order online and have my information circulated in such a bizarre world, but was unable to find one or an address other than Foxy.com. After much soul-searching, I finally filled in all the required forms, made the fatal mouse click, and within minutes received dozens of lascivious emails with offers for things I didn't know were possible for the human body to do.

Finally, The Lelo Egg arrived and is doing wonders for my neuropathy, but the daily assortment of the catalogues, not in plain brown wrappers but in all their perverted, naked glory, has destroyed my reputation. I'm just hoping someone in my building will read this disclaimer and spread the word.

TECHNOLOGY IS *NOT* YOUR FRIEND

What I really wanted for my last birthday was a pair of pajamas, but because they're not digital, I didn't stand a chance. Instead, I was deluged with an arsenal of high-tech "communications breakthrough" gadgets: an iPhone (which I quickly realized was a "not-for-me phone"); a Kindle electronic book (which doesn't feel, smell, or look like a book); and a GPS navigation device (featuring the voice of some irritating woman whom I would never allow in my car, let alone permit her to tell me how to get where I'm going).

I returned the gifts and went to Bloomingdale's to buy my pajamas. Yet what should have been a simple, two-minute transaction was interrupted as my saleslady responded to three text messages and a phone call.

I'm not losing my patience but my sanity. With the wisdom I have gained from age and experience, I have finally decided it's time for all these communications breakthroughs to take a break from breaking through since they're no longer improving communication but actually destroying it.

How?

By making it easier and faster for people everywhere to be in constant contact with each other…about *nothing.*

Nowhere is this more evident than on the social networking sites of which, I'm guessing, there are 375 (which probably jumped to 376 as I was typing "375"). MySpace, Facebook, Twitter, Yuku and any other place inhabited by teens and young singles is not a world where we seniors belong. I learned this fact through personal experience when my ex-wife, Holly, sent me an e-mail, asking me to be her Facebook friend.

As I mentioned before, we had parted amicably decades ago and had remained in casual contact since, but being her Facebook friend felt like a deeper commitment. Just what is a Facebook friend? What are the responsibilities? Are there legal implications?

With some trepidation, I opened the link and there she was, smiling out at me expectantly, with two boxes next to her picture: "Confirm" or "Ignore."

I didn't want to get involved, but how can you ignore someone who's smiling at you and wants to be your friend?

I clicked "Confirm," then briefly logged on to Google to research the side effects of my new acid-reflux medication. When I returned to Facebook, my inbox was bulging with 20 more requests for my friendship, most from people who were already my real-life friends (but apparently that isn't good enough anymore).

With each "Confirm" I clicked, the number of new friends expanded, and within an hour I had more than 50—some of whom were apparently Facebook friends of my Facebook friends, so I couldn't reject them because my friends would think their friends weren't good enough for me. Even worse, there were three messages on my "Wall" (whatever that was) and a space in which, at that time, I was supposed to answer the question, "What are you doing right now?" I was too ashamed to tell the truth ("I'm on Facebook"), so I decided to see what some of my new "friends" were "doing right now".

My daughter said she was drying her hair. Others were

"Watching a rerun of *Seinfeld* in my underwear," "Eating leftover lasagna," "Looking for a clean pair of socks," and "Getting a colonoscopy" (this final one sent from the fellow's BlackBerry). In that moment, I knew exactly what I was "doing right now," and I typed it in: "Leaving Facebook forever."

Tomorrow will bring countless technological breakthroughs, I'm sure. But for my next birthday, I really would like a belt.

FORGOT YOUR PASSWORD?

Yes!!! And so has everyone else as the number of sites keeps growing along with the number of people using them as the number of "takens," and "unavailables" keeps popping up along with the new and insulting "weak."

What does that mean? And who gets to decide?

For 65 web-less years, I had managed to get by with just one password: "Ace Of Aces," as a member of the Tracey Avenue Tigers, a secret society with a hideout constructed of cardboard boxes and an old mattress in my cousin Jerry's basement. It was forgotten until recently when I reached back to a simpler time to register on a new website and was shocked to see "Ace of Aces" was taken; obviously Jerry had succumbed to torture and given it up.

I tried aceofaces1, also taken, and finally was accepted with aceofaces9. It was only a momentary victory because I realized that, along with countless others, it would be forgotten and I'd have go to Forgot Your Password Hell and try to remember the hint: my pet's name, my favorite food, mother's birthday, maiden name, or countless others I have accumulated to the point that I have no idea what hint goes with which password.

In the beginning, it was simple: I was "sillybilly," which worked through five sites. On the sixth, it was taken. I immediately went to "sillybilly1." Finally, at sillybilly4, it was accepted.

Then there was a period of "cute" ones: "bigbucks" for my bank, "clicker" for my cable service, and a few others I can't begin to remember. I sailed along up to "sillybilly10" when I was confronted with a numbers-only site. I started with the year I was born...taken. I shouldn't have been shocked given that 1,989,364 people were born in 1931. (That from a Census Bureau site, no password required.) I added the month... taken. Day, age, address...taken. Finally, my license plate: my accepted password was 193,109,091,303,683.

I never even tried to revisit the site.

I'm sure there is a website to find the average number of passwords needed to function in today's cyber world, but I would need a password to get in, and, with 35, I'm already fighting for my web life. To help, I compiled a password-protected list of the date I made the list, but then I saw the movie *Swordfish* where John Travolta was a computer whiz who could break anyone's passwords since everyone uses birthdays, pets and children's names, so I created one that was so random that no one could figure out...which, of course, includes me.

Things are only going to get worse unless someone comes up with a solution and I think I have it. At birth, in addition to a name, every child should be given a password. It's on a tape recorded by Bob Johnson, the voice on the tapes in the TV series *Mission: Impossible*. To get it, parents have to climb a mountain and memorize it before the tape self-destructs, leaving the parents as the sole possessor of the information. When the child is 13, an appropriate age to be using the Internet responsibly, the parents whisper the password into the child's ear and immediately it is wiped from their memory. This is followed by dinner, dancing, and gifts. If the kid happens to be Jewish, to save money it can be added to the Bar Mitzvah ceremony.

WHEN THE CAT
PEES IN YOUR HAT

…is it time to say "that is that?"

Where is Dr. Seuss when you need him?

As all who own pets will understand—and those who don't, never will—how much do you endure and spend before putting the family pet to sleep?

"To sleep"—a comforting euphemism which makes the decision seem less final, as if you can change your mind and wake him.

My wife, Joanna, and I are at that point with 20-year-old Bart, "the cat who peed in my hat," the latest pit stop since his loss of direction, instincts, and common decency in finding his litter box (actually box*es* as we now have three strategically placed at new locations he has marked for his relief but not ours).

When you factor in the countless bottles of sprays and potions—Pee No More, Boundaries, Miracle Stain and Odor Remover, and Kitty Pads—our apartment is beginning to look a lot like a display case at PETCO.

I can hear the chorus of, "He's only a *cat!"* and I know there are more important issues to occupy our thoughts and concerns, more meaningful places to spend our money and time. But this is Bart we're talking about, the four-month-old matted clump of fur I found rummaging through the garbage at a house we rented in St. Bart's one Christmas. I made the mistake of feeding him a saucer of milk, a snack that has thus far cost us about $20,000. He adopted me before I did him, becoming my irresistible and constant companion for the next two weeks: following me everywhere, curling up on my lap wherever I sat, and endearing himself to my family. So, when it was time for us to leave, how could we abandon this helpless loving creature to the garbage pile of life? After a $300 trip to the local vet for shots and a certificate of health, he was cleared for the trip to his new home in New York.

I quickly realized this furry phony had planned the whole thing from that first saucer of milk, and to this day, he continues to charm and manipulate his way into everyone's heart. People who hate cats love Bart. Joanna, who is allergic to cats, falls asleep reading with his paw marking her place, and wakes red-eyed and sneezing but insistent that Bart and she need that time together. He had a trouble-free run for about 15 years, the normal lifespan for a cat.

But this is Bart we're talking about, and as he pushes the limits of life expectancy and our common sense gets pushed right along with it, the costs, financial and emotional, are never ending.

His heart problem, which is controlled by two pills a day administered with scratching, gagging, and spitting out in various locations found at random, has cost about $4,000 to date. The underactive thyroid treated with a nuclear iodine injection and quarantine for 10 days was $5,000. Arthritis—diagnosis, x-rays and medications, another $2,000. Dentistry? (He only has two teeth left) $1,500.

Now, the carpet and upholstery cleaning, and the inconvenience of closing off various rooms of the apartment are reaching a point of absurdity.

It gets down to a quality of life issue: his and ours.